SUCCESS STORIES FOR YOUNG PROFESSIONALS

EXCEEDING EXPECTATIONS

Mastering the Seven Keys to Professional Success

Scott Weighart

First Edition

ISBN 0-9621264-4-6
ISBN-13 (effective January 2007) 978-0-9621264-4-4

Printed in the United States of America

For El,
partner in everything

CONTENTS

ACKNOWLEDGEMENTS

Although this book's concept has been in the making for several years, the actual creation of *Exceeding Expectations* occurred at amazing speed. This would not have been possible without the efforts of quite a few individuals.

First and foremost, I have to thank the students and alumni who were amazingly responsive when I asked them to step up and contribute their stories. Keith Laughman, Ali Ciccariello, Genevieve Jewell, Sharon Kim, Molly Simpson, and Amanda O'Brien made life easy for me by writing up stories themselves, but I also am indebted to Michelle George, Amanda Roche, Sean Jones, Ron Ordell, Amy Black, Chris Wright, Aviad Benzikry, Greg Fischer, Tyler Harvey, Sky-Lynn Priddle, and Anthony Caines for agreeing to be interviewed for the book. I also want to thank Dan Ely, Tony Lam, David LeClair, Kristin Poole, Bill Mayo, and Caleb Ginsberg for signing off on their stories and correcting my memory at times.

Many cooperative education professionals played a vital role in this book's development as well. I am especially grateful to Mary Rose Tichar from Case Western Reserve University, as she wrote up four stories about her students for these pages. In addition, I thank Olaf Paese at the University of Waterloo as well as Jennifer Rubin and Rita Crane from Drexel University: They steered me toward some great performers at their programs, and their interviews add a great element to the book. As for employers,

Barbara Murphy of The Gillette Company was quick to step up and offer assistance. At Northeastern, newly retired coordinator Bill Sloane wrote an epic piece about his own co-op from over 30 years ago. Charlie Bognanni did the heavy lifting on a few stories, and I also received great contributions from Jacki Diani, Mary Carney, and Lisa Foster. Another retiree—Mike Ablove—found his way into the book with some great stories. Mary Kane gave the manuscript a final review before we went to print.

I asked a great deal of former Northeastern University president John Curry as well as some of my top alums—Jennifer Merrill, Guy Doyon, and Dan Belcher. They were charged with reading the whole manuscript and writing up blurbs that could be used for the back cover and in promoting the book, and some of them had only a week to do it! I'm very appreciative of this critical contribution. My writer friend Scott Campbell also read the manuscript very quickly and yet did a thorough and thoughtful job in offering suggestions.

Thanks also to those who have brought this book a long way in terms of its appearance. Raphael Bueno came up with the title. On very short notice, Robin Friedman of Visual Velocity designed the book's front and back cover and did a terrific job. Jill Gómez and Kate Poverman came to our rescue with proofreading when we very much needed it. Lastly, and most significantly, my wife Ellie showed great versatility in editing and desktop publishing the book while juggling many other responsibilities. Thanks to all.

Scott Weighart
July 2006

INTRODUCTION

Back in 1991, I did some consulting work for a company that was hired by many businesses that were looking to improve their training and development programs. Basically, the idea was to interview many of each client's top performers, focusing on "critical incidents" in their roles with that organization. Asked to talk about their best and/or most challenging experiences, these exceptional performers walked through everything they were thinking, feeling, and doing as the situations unfolded and ultimately resolved.

My usual job was to help analyze the interview transcripts to try to figure out what behavioral competencies were demonstrated through those true stories—traits such as cross-functional awareness, out-of-the-box thinking, and relationship-building. We would keep at it until we had covered every element of what differentiated these outstanding employees.

For one project, I came up with an idea to write up the most compelling interview examples as true mini-cases to help trainees understand what those behavioral traits *really* looked like in action instead of just presenting them as abstract concepts. One senior consultant described my packet of cases as the single best element of a whole series of deliverables for that client.

Fifteen years later, I decided to utilize a similar approach to create this book. For those who are unfamiliar with the concept of "cooperative education," it a form of higher education in which students combine academic studies with very substantial work in a professional environment in order to gain job experience, test out a career, and to make connections in the professionals world. As a member of the cooperative education faculty at Northeastern University, I help students with all activities related to a job search as well as ensuring that they are successful on the job and in processing their experiences after returning to the classroom environment. Typically, our students complete a typical freshman year and then alternate repeatedly between six months of full-time work and six months of classes.

Reflecting on over a decade of experience in helping young professionals succeed through this program, I wrote up dozens of stories that would inspire and inform aspiring professionals as well as the educators who help them make the transition from classroom to workplace. Many are stories that students in my Professional Development for Co-op course have enjoyed hearing over the years. Then I reached out to some of my top alums, my colleagues at Northeastern and at several other co-op schools, asking people for either great stories or for the contact information for great performers. In the latter case, I conducted critical incident interviews with the individuals.

I ended up with roughly 85 short stories, all revolving around how to be successful in the workplace. In many cases, I have changed the names of the students involved and omitted organization names: Even if the stories were positive, I didn't want to include individual's names unless I had written permission. Some people preferred to be anonymous, and I was unable to track down some of my alums who graduated many years ago.

As I wrote each story, I noted several possible themes that the story might be used to represent—tracking all of the stories and themes in an Excel spreadsheet. By the time I finished compiling stories, I had 15 to 20 different themes. But some clearly overlapped—

"making sacrifices" seemed to be a component of the larger theme of "seeing the big picture;" "assuming the best" was really the same as "staying positive" and so on. Thus the next step was to boil down the number of themes until I had as few as possible while still having an appropriate category for each story.

I ended up with seven themes. They are as follows:

1. Own Responsibility
2. Stay Positive
3. Exceed Expectations
4. Do The Right Thing
5. See The Big Picture
6. Control What You Can
7. Build Relationships

Most of the stories were great examples of at least one—and in some cases several—of these seven themes. I sorted the stories accordingly, putting each one into the category that it *best* represented. In the end, I think you'll agree that a young professional in any field who can display these seven qualities consistently will be well on their way to getting their career off to a fantastic start.

In my previous book, *Find Your First Professional Job*, the primary focus is on getting that first job and on preventing problems from arising once you have it. As the title indicates, *Exceeding Expectations* concentrates on what it takes to get to the next level: The focus is on striving toward professional excellence.

Working with young professionals, I often tell them to do things like "own responsibility" or to "stay positive" in a job. However, these are abstract concepts—especially for someone who may have little or no concrete experience working in a professional environment.

My hope is that any young, aspiring professional who reads the true stories that exemplify these themes will start to understand what it *really* means to exceed expectations in the workplace. Exceeding expectations is one of the seven themes, but it also is a great term for capturing what this book is all about. By learning what it takes to be an outstanding professional in these seven ways, you will start to see that great success and personal fulfillment are definitely within your grasp.

Professional success is not magic: It is based on hard work combined with an appreciation of what differentiates star performers from those who merely are content to show up at work each day.

If you're willing to provide the hard work, I believe that this book will help give you that appreciation of what it takes to excel. You may not have any previous professional experience, or you may have had some opportunities to do serious work in a meaningful, career-related role. Either way, there is always more to learn when it comes to *Exceeding Expectations*.

Scott Weighart
June 2006

CHAPTER ONE

Own Responsibility

Over the last two decades, I have taught everything from kindergarteners through college seniors. I have taught Organizational Behavior courses to hundreds of students at Boston University and Northeastern University, and by now I've worked with thousands of students in my role as a cooperative education faculty member at Northeastern for over 11 years.

That said, my most difficult day as an educator occurred when I was 24 and working as a substitute teacher in several Boston Public Schools. I had been very fortunate in this role: Within a week of starting, a terrific elementary school in Mission Hill snapped me up to be their "building substitute teacher." This meant that almost every day, I went to the same school to provide coverage for absences—and it was a very pleasant place to work.

However, if no one was absent on a given day, sometimes our principal had to inform the powers-that-be that his building substitute was available for duty elsewhere. As luck would have it, this happened on a morning when I had debated taking a day off because of a final exam that was scheduled in one of my business school courses that night. Ultimately I had figured I'd probably go to my usual school and get a little downtime during which I could study. But when the phone rang before 7 a.m. that morning, there was no way I could beg out.

Being a substitute is always a little daunting: You get a call and within an hour you have to figure out how to get to the school and make the commute without knowing what you're going to be asked to do. On one other occasion, I had shown up at 7:50, and the principal quickly walked me to the classroom. He told me that I'd be teaching bilingual first grade and asked if I knew any Spanish. "Very little," I admitted. "Just do the best you can," he said. And I got through a day, learning a little Spanish and employing some of the more bilingual students to help with translation.

But that was nothing compared to what I faced on my toughest day. About the only good news was that I could teach in English. Otherwise, it was a tough draw: I had a big class of fourth graders, most of whom were tough kids from inner-city projects. Even worse, it was an "open school," with few walls, so it was clear that any trouble that I had in controlling the kids would be obvious to the neighboring classroom.

The morning began with two kids sprinting into the room and sliding into their desks as if they were going into second base. "What are you doing?" I said. They just laughed at me. It was one of those rooms where the kids just love having a sub, as it was an opportunity to see how much they could get away with.

They proceeded to push my buttons every way imaginable. They were rude to me and to each other. A few kids got into physical tussles or verbal conflicts with each other. Most of them seemed angry or indifferent. In response, I tried every tactic I could think of to get them to engage them in the work at hand. I attempted humor, positive reinforcement, warnings, threats, you name it. I told them that if they would behave and focus on their work, then I would tell them the story about the time I interviewed rap musicians Run-DMC in my days as a college journalist.

Nothing seemed to work. I could distract them for small bits of time but couldn't really sustain an environment that was going to be educational. After two or three hours, I resorted to a desperation tactic. "We're going outside for Phys Ed," I told them.

"But we don't have gym today," a few complained.

"We do now," I said. Once I got them outside, I made them a deal. We were going to run wind sprints, and I would run with them. I told them that if any single one of them could beat me—even once—in a sprint, then I would allow them to do whatever they wanted in the classroom for the rest of the day—play games, fool around, whatever. "But if no one is able to beat me, then you have to listen to me and work the rest of the day."

We proceeded to run about 11 or 12 wind sprints. I made sure the races were all close, letting them take the lead and just nipping them in the last ten yards each time. Finally they had had enough, and we went back inside.

I didn't really believe that they would live up to their end of the bargain when it came to listening to me as a result of losing. But at worst I figured that they might be too tired to give me much trouble. Sure enough, they were relatively peaceful for the next hour or two.

By the early afternoon, though, they were just as annoying and difficult as they had been first thing in the morning. I kept after them, but by the time the day came to a merciful end, I had to admit to myself that we really had accomplished very little in terms of getting any work done. I was exhausted and depressed.

The students went home, and I sat at the teacher's desk, getting my things together. Just then the teacher from the classroom next door came into the room and introduced herself, and I did the same.

She looked puzzled. "What was going on in here today?" she said, seeming to be genuinely curious.

"I apologize for the noise level," I said. "I hope it wasn't too much of a distraction for you. I tried everything I could to keep the kids in line, but ultimately I failed."

"No, you don't understand," she said. "That's the best behaved they've been all year."

I went home feeling a strange mixture of a little pride combined with a deepening sense of depression. So it was a good day for that group, perhaps. It still was a bad day by my standards. To this day I believe that there are other things I could have done to make it a very good day as opposed to a less horrible than usual day.

This is because I believe so strongly that any professional needs to own responsibility when it comes to what happens in the workplace. Once you start believing that a situation is impossible, that's exactly what it becomes.

The First Key – Own Responsibility

The first key to professional success is to own responsibility. Epictetus, a Roman philosopher who was born a slave, said the following:

"Circumstances do not rise to meet our expectations. Events happen as they do. People behave as they are. Embrace what you actually get."

He also said:

"When something happens, the only thing in your power is your attitude toward it; you can either accept it or resent it. What really frightens and dismays us is not external events themselves, but the way in which we think about them. It is not things that disturb us, but our interpretation of their significance."

In other words, what matters in any situation is what is in the eye of the beholder: Perception becomes reality. As automotive entrepreneur Henry Ford once said, "Either you think you can or you can't; either way you're right."

I'm sure that you have known friends or family members, classmates or co-workers who seem to live under a dark cloud. When they face a challenge or difficulty, an inconvenience or test, they see it as proof that the world is an unfair, unjust place, or that people or events are somehow conspiring to make them miserable. It's not *their* fault: They have what psychologists call an "external locus of control." Things happen *to* these people.

But then I'm equally certain that you have known individuals who are just the opposite: Even when life deals them a tough hand of cards, they play it to the best of their ability. When they face complications or changes, they manage to relish the challenge and seize the opportunity for something positive to come out of it. And if things don't work out, they don't blame anyone else: They are accountable for mistakes and determined to learn from them. These people have an "internal locus of control." These people *make* things happen!

Elements of Owning Responsibility

In analyzing many stories that had themes related to owning responsibility, I was able to identify several elements that comprise this key to professional success:

1. *"It's not the situation; it's how you handle it."*
This is a favorite expression of some employers I work with regularly through my role in cooperative education at Northeastern University. The idea is that you certainly will encounter obstacles in your career, and they likely will come sooner rather than later. These obstacles can take many forms: Maybe you'll be saddled with an unreasonable boss or an incompetent and/or unmotivated co-worker. Perhaps you won't have the best resources or what you believe to be an adequate amount of time to do the right thing the right way. Ultimately, though, you need to make up your mind that you will not let these obstacles derail you on your career path.

2. *Offer explanations, not excuses.*
When something goes wrong, you need to communicate honestly about what has happened. If that means acknowledging an oversight or error on your part, you need to do so and accept the consequences. Don't go out of your way to blame or undermine others: Stick to facts and let people draw their own conclusions about the rest. Give credit–and take it, if appropriate–for successes, and be accountable for failures as well.

3. *Acknowledge your limitations.*
A quote of uncertain origin (although sometimes attributed to author Mark Twain) is the following: "Better to keep your mouth closed and thought a fool than to open it and remove all doubt." Many people live by that principle, but it's a potentially dangerous philosophy. Owning responsibility means that you sometimes need to ask questions or admit when you don't have the answers—even though doing either can be uncomfortable. The biggest mistakes often happen when people either do the right thing the wrong way OR the wrong thing the right way–simply because they made assumptions about what to do when they were afraid to ask.

When you're a developing professional, it takes time to figure out exactly *when* is the most opportune time to ask a question and *who* should be asked. Likewise, if you have to ask the same question repeatedly, then you need a better system of keeping track of the answers! But you can't let pride or embarrassment prevent you from speaking up when you're not sure what to do.

4. Be someone who makes things happen, rather than one of the people who seem to have things happen to them.
At Northeastern, I tend to get very few complaints from the employers who hire our students. That said, the most common gripe is that students can't get to work on time. When I talk to students who have ongoing tardiness problems, though, it's very rare for someone just to admit that they simply did not live up to their responsibility by doing whatever it takes to get to work on time. Instead, these people seem to see themselves as victims of cruel fate. They blame the public transportation system, or traffic, or the fact that the job is not as exciting as they hoped it would be.

If that perception doesn't change, then there is little hope that this problem will go away. These are people who just can't or won't take charge of their destiny. I liken them to a sprinter who runs up to a hurdle and thinks, "Hmm... That's just too high" and basically gives up. People who own responsibility find ways to get over, under, or around the hurdles that arise in their careers.

Most importantly, I find that people who own responsibility inevitably are happier individuals. If you really believe that you have no control over your fate, then it doesn't really matter whether you expend more energy or not. Why bother, if you don't believe you can make a difference? The challenge is that it's easy to underestimate the degree to which you *can* make a difference when you decide to own responsibility and do whatever it takes to overcome adversity to be successful.

True Stories about Owning Responsibility

The Victim Mentality

Like any other member of the cooperative education faculty at Northeastern University, I have numerous responsiblities. With students, I assist with career counseling, resume writing, interview strategy, the job search process, and providing guidance and assistance while they are working as well as in making the transition back to the classroom.

I also work with employers, helping them with every aspect of hiring and managing our young employees. When possible, I try to get out in the field to better understand each organization and how our students might succeed as employees. Sometimes, though, employers come to our campus to conduct interviews. Either way, the variety of employer insights that I get to hear is invaluable.

For several years, "Stan Trevor"—a Director in the Information Technology Group at a Fortune 500 company—came on campus to interview our students for co-op positions. One of the great things about Stan's visits was that I inevitably came away with great "teachable moments" that I subsequently could share with students.

For many interview cycles, Stan was known for his quirky, brain-teasing interview questions. Here are some favorites that I recall:

- How would you make a cheesecake for the Queen of England?
- How would you take an aircraft engine apart and put it back together again?
- How many turtles would you need to make turtle soup?

Some of these questions just about made my candidates wet

their pants—and not from laughing. However, the questions are not as odd as they seem: If you substitute the words "software application" for "cheesecake" in the first question, it becomes comparatively easy.

In any event, Stan came to Boston again a few years ago for interviews. Knowing he seldom repeated questions, I asked him if he had any new brain-teasers for the candidates.

"Well, I do have some problem-solving questions, but I'm moving away from the brain-teasers," he told me. "More and more, I look at the interview process as a way of rooting out individuals who have a victim mentality."

Stan proceeded to explain. In interviewing full-time candidates, he often came across individuals who claimed that they would've/should've/could've accomplished great things in their last job. The problem, they would say, was that they lacked adequate resources... or productive colleagues... or competent supervisors.

Stan would say to himself: "At our company, we have great resources, terrific colleagues, and great mentoring and supervision. This person will be a star for us: We just have to get him or her in to the right setting."

But things didn't turn out that way with these hires. Often in a matter of months, they were pointing fingers at something or someone that supposedly was keeping them from reaching their full potential. Looking into these situations, Stan eventually concluded that the real problem was that he had hired people who have a "victim mentality."

Stan and other managers at his company are the inspiration for that expression that I noted earlier in this chapter: "It's not the situation; it's how you handle it." Eventually in your career—and perhaps sooner than later—you are going to run into an incompetent boss, a dysfunctional team, a hostile co-worker, or some other form of roadblock. Are you going to let your career be derailed because of these obstacles, or are you going to find a way to succeed regardless?

We all know individuals who see the glass as half-empty... or maybe half-full of poison! In their world of woe, these cynics expect things to be bad... and so they are.

Even if you have a natural tendency toward pessimism, do whatever you can to avoid the "victim mentality." Maybe you're the kind of person who expects the worst, but try to use that as a positive by doing whatever you can to succeed even if the worst-case scenario arises. The saddest thing about this world view is that people like this go through life not even realizing how much their own low expectations actually make things worse for themselves. Acknowledge problems, but work toward jumping over those hurdles instead of complaining about how high they appear to be.

Earning the Learning

Increasingly, young professionals entering the workforce often have extremely high expectations about what they will be able to accomplish in their first jobs. In some ways, that's great... but it can be a problem if the individual doesn't have realistic expectations. We frequently see that, unfortunately. In the last cycle, my colleague Bill Munze worked with several entrepreneurship students who wanted very advanced positions in the real estate field. Bill would try to explain that they would need to prove themselves first in lower-level positions, but some of these people just could not accept that. If these students wouldn't change their attitude, it made for some painful lessons—usually in the form of a long, unsuccessful job search.

My co-op colleague Lisa Foster works with students in a few different majors related to the health sciences. She passed along a story that aptly fit this theme. "Henry" was hired by one of the many exceptional hospital facilities in the Boston area. He was really excited: He wanted to be able to observe surgeries. However, he was not hired to do that. Various basic administrative duties comprised his job, including the filing of medical records. Instead of focusing on doing that as efficiently and effectively as possible, he put it off. He repeatedly tried to get the attention of surgeons as they hurried through the facility's hallways, asking if he could observe them in surgery. "Yeah, yeah, yeah..." was the usual distracted response. "Talk to your supervisor about it."

Of course, asking his supervisor was a problem. Henry honestly believed that the filing work was beneath him; he didn't see the importance of doing what they were paying him to do. And he was under the impression that people would come to him if and when they needed help on administrative tasks. So when he wasn't trying to corral a surgeon, he spent a lot of time reading magazines on the sly.

Ultimately he was fired—a humiliating experience for him. Fortunately, it was a wake-up call: He is now with another employer and is a great fit. He finally got the message that first and foremost you need to prove yourself when you're asked to do anything in a job.

The Credibility Bank Account

One day NU student "Tara Isaacson" was frantic going into the office. The subway had broken down, and her cellphone would not work underground. Stuck for almost an hour and a half, she knew that she was going to be very late. That had never happened before, and she felt awful about it.

Finally the subway got moving, and she dashed from the station into work. Before anyone could say anything, she immediately told her manager and the other full-time workers what had happened. "The 'T' broke down! I was stuck for over an hour!

I'm really sorry I'm late!"

Much to her surprise, everyone started laughing. She was confused until her manager explained. "A few minutes ago, I was telling everyone that the subway system must have come to a complete halt if Tara is late!" he said. "And I was right!!" Not only was it a non-issue, everyone had a good laugh about it.

I tell students that story now before they go out on their first co-op. The moral of it is that once in a great while there might be a completely legitimate reason why you would be late to work. But then I ask them how it would have gone over if Tara typically had been late once or twice a week for the first four months in that job. The result would have been an uncomfortable silence and a sense of "here we go again."

Credibility with an employer is like a bank account. If you make deposits on a regular basis, you can afford an occasional withdrawal. Likewise, if you are a great performer who consistently engages in professional behaviors, you will find that people are much more understanding if you really are sick or have to be late for some reason.

Mistakes Happen

Finance co-op student Amanda Roche had just made a disturbing discovery: She had made a pretty major mistake on a cost report that already had been submitted for processing. Even worse, she had seen how her overwhelmed boss had reacted when others had made similar errors. However, she also had taken note of how those people had chosen to deal with the situation, and that had given her some insight into understanding her boss. "I had seen him get frustrated at other people," she recalls. "But people would just wait at their desks, waiting for him to figure it out. He would blow up: 'What do you think you're doing?' he'd say, things like that."

Although she felt really nervous about it and certain that he would yell at her, Amanda decided to be proactive about it. "I was sure he would blow up, but before he could, I marched into his office," Amanda says. "I wanted to let you know that I made a mistake on this project," she told him. She proceeded to explain what she had done, why the error had occurred, and what she proposed to do to remedy the situation. "I want to apologize; it won't happen again," she added.

Much to her surprise, his attitude immediately softened. "Mistakes happen," he said. "There are so many reports that we have to send to different countries," he told her.

"He also liked the idea I had about how to fix it," Amanda says. "We went over the corrected report on the phone with the customer, and I offered to stay late to help make it happen."

It turned to be a great lesson for her. "The fact that I was the first one to bring it up and show how we were going to move forward made a big difference," she reported. "He wasn't able to bite my head off."

Fired During The Last Week Of Work

It's not easy to get fired with one week left in a six-month co-op job, but "Keith Harford" managed to do it. To his credit, though, he walked into my office one weekday morning shortly before Christmas and quickly said, "You're not going to be happy with me today."

Keith proceeded to explain exactly what had happened. A few days before, his boss had pulled him aside. He told Keith that the company was going to have a holiday party. "Alcohol will be served at the party, and I know you're not 21," the manager said. "This is a liability issue for the company. So you have two choices: You can come to the party and not drink, or you can decide that you wouldn't be comfortable attending the party under the circumstances. I'm completely fine with whatever you choose."

Well, you can guess what happened. Keith went to the party, and some of the full-time workers offered to get drinks for him. "Hey, it's Christmas!" they said. "What's the harm in having a beer or two? You're not driving, right?" They cajoled Keith a bit, and he ended up having a few drinks. His boss found out before the party ended and terminated him on the spot. It happened the night before, and Keith came to tell me the very next morning.

Keith could have blamed his co-workers, but he didn't. "I was told upfront very directly that I couldn't drink, and I did, so I have to accept the consequences," he told me. "I'm so angry at myself right now: The co-op was almost over, but they had already promised to keep me on working part-time during classes at $15/hour... and I really need that money."

I could have done a number of things at that point—failing him for co-op, referring him to our Judicial Affairs for consuming alcohol, and so forth. Instead, I told him that I was sorry that it happened but that I respected the fact that he owned the responsibility for it. "It's a painful lesson," I said. "As far as I'm concerned, you'll learn something from this, and we'll move forward with referrals for you next time." There wasn't much more to say.

Within an hour, the employer called, sounding angry and thinking that he was about to break this news of the termination to me. He calmed down considerably when he learned that Keith took the initiative to tell me what had happened and that he had done so with complete accuracy. Keith had not pointed fingers at his co-workers, so the manager was surprised to hear that they had played a role in this. It didn't change the outcome, but I could tell the manager respected how Keith had taken responsibility for his actions.

Culture Clash

When working with aspiring professionals, I find that some of them are mystified when I tell them that they will learn many important things on co-op that have nothing to do with Management Information Systems or Supply Chain Management. For example, a co-op or internship can teach you a great deal about what kind of work environment is best for you, as this story by my co-op colleague Charlie Bognanni reveals. Being successful as a professional means learning how to adapt to different supervisors and work cultures as well as mastering the technical elements of your job.

On his first co-op, "Andrew Karlini" had worked in the accounting department at Morris Foods, a large restaurant chain. He loved his job, learned a great deal, and received an excellent evaluation. While meeting with Andrew, I learned that in addition to the accounting experience he gained, he particularly liked the work culture at Morris.

"It's very laid-back," I can remember him saying. "Don't get me wrong: We work hard and get our work done, but basically there are very few rules about what time we have to be in, when we take lunch, or even when we go home. The attitude is: Get the work done; we don't worry about the other stuff." Andrew mentioned that he flourished in a work culture that allowed him that kind of autonomy.

For his next co-op assignment, Andrew wanted a change in venue and had expressed interest in working in a financial institution. He was able to land a job as a financial analyst with "LCB, Inc.," a major investment company in downtown Boston. Both Andrew and I were confident he would do well. After all, he was smart, dedicated, and industrious. There was one feature, however, about this new company that neither Andrew nor I focused on: It had a completely different work culture from the restaurant chain.

About a month into his job with LCB I received a phone call from the Human Resources Manager at LCB. She was very concerned about Andrew. Although the actual work he was performing was fine, they were distressed about his ability to follow rules and company policy. More specifically, he was coming to work late, taking lunch hours at unorthodox times, and dressing a bit too casually. Andrew's argument was that he was still working the expected 40 hours per week (he was staying late to make up for his tardiness), not extending his lunch time, and dressing the way he did at Morris. The argument was not accepted by LCB. They explained to Andrew that although he didn't agree with the rules, he had to abide by them or there would be disciplinary action.

Here's what happened: Andrew's manager at LCB developed some very detailed and explicit rules he had to follow. It worked. Andrew had become so used to a laissez-faire work environment that it took direction and very specific guidelines to help him adjust.

After completing his co-op, Andrew admitted that it took him some time to adjust to LCB's work culture. "I just wasn't ready for it," Andrew said. "I had become so entrenched in Morris' work environment and culture that it took a while to learn new rules. I never really grew to like it, but I knew that in order to survive at LCB I would have to adjust to their culture. It wasn't always fun and sometimes downright painful but I did it."

"Down the road, I think I prefer a work culture closer to that of Morris than what I experienced at LCB."

The Borderline Candidate

I have many co-ops who work at Microsoft, and getting the right combination of personality, passion for technology, and willingness to relocate over 3,000 miles is always a challenge. After working with them for several interview cycles, Microsoft eventually let me decide who would go on their interview schedule.

I always aim to give them the best possible candidates.

One day Dave LeClair came to my office and asked me if he could be on the interview schedule when Microsoft came to town in a few weeks. I told him that I wasn't sure. He had no corporate experience, having done his previous two co-ops in academic environments. His grades were nothing special, and his technical skills were pretty ordinary. He also was a middler—a third-year student in our five-year program—and he would be able to interview next year if not now. I told him I would give him consideration but that, at best, he was "on the bubble" to get an interview. He said, "Okay," and we left it at that.

A few days after that, Dave came back into my office. "Look, I respect the fact that it's your decision regarding who gets on that interview schedule, and I'll live with whatever you decide," Dave said. "But I just wanted to make sure I get on the table why I think I would be a good person to put on the schedule.

"If I got the job, I would view it as the opportunity of a lifetime. I would be willing to commit to doing both of my last two co-ops there." Speaking with real passion, he went on to explain how much conviction he had about this being right for him and how he could be right for them.

On the spot, I gave him a slot on the interview schedule and told him that Microsoft loves to see passion for technology as well as people who very badly want to work there and who are likely to be converted to full-time hires after graduation.

Dave didn't disappoint me. Not only did he get the job, he proved to be a leader when we had our meeting of new co-op hires. He admitted to the group that he was excited but nervous about whether he would have what it takes to succeed, given how much was at stake. That set the stage for a very open and honest dialogue, helping others to admit their own anxieties about the imminent co-op.

He was a great performer out in Washington for two co-ops and landed a full-time job with the company after graduation. Not bad for a guy who marginally made the cut for his first interview! It's hard to overestimate the value of drive and intensity.

The Unwritten Rules

I got a call from one of my biggest employers several years ago; they were having trouble with "Neil Parker," one of my co-ops. There were various symptoms, but the underlying cause was that Neil was doing a really poor job of figuring out the unwritten rules of the workplace.

The employer had a flextime policy, so Neil thought it would be okay to show up at 7:45 one day, then 9:30 the next... and he would leave no later than 5 p.m., regardless of when he arrived. The written policy didn't say so, but the unwritten understanding was that it was okay to start work earlier or later, but that you should basically pick a regular start time and stick with it. This was explained to Neil, who apparently had forgotten this.

When I discussed this with him, I asked him why he thought it was okay to come in as late as 9:30. "Well, there are a lot of full-time employees on my floor who regularly come in at 10, 10:30, sometimes even later," Neil said. "No one seems to have any problem with that."

I asked his manager about this. It turned out that the people coming in after 10 were not in Neil's group: They were software developers who worked independently. In Neil's job, everyone had to work together. For another thing, the developers often preferred to work well into the evening, often staying after 8 p.m.—well after Neil skipped out at 5. As long as the developers were working an eight-hour day and meeting their goals, *their* boss was fine with their hours. Neil's boss understandably had an issue with him coming in at 9:30, taking an hour for lunch, and then leaving at 5. That's a 6 ½ hour day.

It can be helpful to observe the behavior of others in determining what might be "okay" behavior at a company, but you have to be careful about concluding something is okay just because someone else is doing it! You might be imitating behavior that is unethical. As in this case, you also just might not have all the information.

Late To Bed, Late To Rise

Although the vast majority of the stories in this book are positive ones, some horror stories can be instructive as well. Here is the all-time champion when it comes to a student who *fails* to own responsibility. I'll disguise the name of the student as well as the school he attended to protect the innocent... and the guilty party!

"Simon Van Winkle" was a business student who had managed to obtain an out-of-state co-op job in a financial company. Several weeks into his job, Simon consistently began to show up late to work. And it was more than a little late: More often than not, Simon would come in at 11:15, 11:30, even noon—and it was a typical corporate 9-to-5 environment. He never called in advance to say that he would be late, and he apparently saw no reason to provide any explanation upon arrival.

Naturally, his supervisor pulled him aside for a little chat after this had been going on for some time. "Why are you getting in so late?" he asked.

"Oh, right, I'm sorry about that," Simon said. "It's just that I have a new girlfriend."

The manager was confused. "A new girlfriend?"

"Yeah," Simon said. "Well, one thing leads to another, and we just seem to end up staying up *really* late. It's just really hard to get out of bed in the morning."

Not believing his ears, the manager asked, "You mean to tell me you're getting here at 11:30 or 12 just because you have a new *girlfriend*?"

"Well, that's not the only reason," Simon said. "I'm also a smoker, and this is a smoke-free environment. So I do get here usually by 11:15 or 11:30, but then I have to have a cigarette before I come inside."

As you might imagine, the manager terminated him shortly thereafter. But the story gets better. Upon getting the word that he was no longer employed, Simon was outraged that his boss would fire him for such a reason. So he went to his boss's boss—the Chief Financial Officer of the company—to complain about this "unfair treatment."

To put it as politely as I can, her response was something along the lines of "Kid, don't let the door hit you on the butt on the way out." Even then the audacity of his behavior never seemed to occur to him. He called his co-op coordinator back at his school to whine about how badly the company treated its co-ops, relating his whole tale of woe with complete honesty—which was about the only thing he had going for him, obviously.

Mixed-up Envelopes

"Sherrie," a Class of 2002 graduate from the College of Arts and Sciences at Northeastern University, is now well on her way to becoming a lawyer. As she shows in this story, there are some jobs in which there is almost no such thing as a small mistake. But by proactively and thoroughly owning responsibility for an honest error, she saved the day—and maybe her job.

In my early paralegal days in a domestic relations law firm, I once mixed up the envelopes of documents going to two separate clients. Fortunately, they were not adverse parties, nor was it communication going to opposing counsel or official documents to the court. The snafu came to light when our client called my boss—one of the founding partners of the firm—and chuckled about the fact that the letter he mistakenly received indicated he would have visitation rights with children. He was childless, in fact.

I knew paralegals who had been fired in the past for lesser mistakes. I immediately walked into my boss's office. I sat down, looked him straight in the eye, and told him what must have happened: It was just an accidental, end-of-the-day slipup. I also said I knew the seriousness of the infraction: Essentially, it could be considered to be malpractice. And I apologized. I told him I would call both affected clients to explain the mistake, and that I would take this as a lesson to be more scrupulous in the future. The partner knew from my face that I was serious, and more importantly, genuine. I kept my job.

Internet Trouble

As technology evolves, it leads to new opportunities... and to potential pitfalls for young professionals. At Northeastern, we teach a course called Professional Development for Co-op, in which students about to embark upon their first co-op job learn the fundamentals about resume-writing, interviewing, and on-the-job performamnce. The last time I taught this class, a heated debate erupted about how technology can work against you during a job search.

While I was lecturing about what should be included on a resume, someone asked a pretty innocuous question: "Why aren't we encouraged to put photos on our resumes? After all, I've heard that employers look up job candidates on Facebook and myspace."

That question was quickly shouted down. "Wait a second," one young woman said. "Employers look at Facebook? That's NOT

FAIR! They're not supposed to look at that!" Quite a few students in my class seemed alarmed and almost betrayed upon learning that a potential employer could view what they had posted online.

For those who are "technologically challenged" and therefore unfamiliar with these terms, I should explain. "Facebook" and "myspace" are websites that have experienced an incredible surge in popularity among college students over the last several years. You can look at them at www.facebook.com or www.myspace.com if so inclined.

Anyone with a university e-mail address can create a profile on Facebook. With some exceptions, a user can only see online profiles of individuals from their own university. Typically, college students or young alumni post all kinds of information about themselves: photos, hobbies, messages, and so forth. It can be a useful way to meet people who share interests or to learn more about a classmate who you may have met casually. As for myspace, anyone at all can create a profile... and anyone with a computer can view it!

So why all the outrage and concern in my class about employers seeing this? Well, using my neu.edu e-mail address, I created a profile and looked up the students in my class. Sure enough, I saw all kinds of information that these students would not want a hiring employer to see. One mild-mannered accounting student belonged to an online interest group called "I LOVE PORN." One of the top marketing students in my class had photos of herself passed out drunk in various places. Quite a few had profanity, sexual references, and "true confessions" about guys and gals and celebrities they liked.

While many employers don't have a university e-mail account, they still could ask their current co-op student or anyone else with a university connection to look up a job applicant on Facebook.

As for myspace, that's even more open. Checking Google for one student with an unusual name, I was startled to see that her myspace page was the first search result. I clicked on it and promptly heard an incredibly raunchy parody of a Beach Boys song. A friend of hers had posted it on my student's message board, and the song launched automatically as soon as anyone opened her profile! If she really felt a need to have such a profile, couldn't she have used a pseudonym at least?

When the issue arose in class, what amazed me most was the notion that many of my students found it "unfair" that employers might see these lascivious words and photos. It was as if they viewed the Internet as a cozy, private club instead of an incredibly public venue.

Since then, the issue has continued to hit the fan. In May 2006, we had an employer rescind a job offer based on some derogatory things the prospective hire had said about the interviewing process in her online blog. Some of my older students told me that they had seen employers check out people online, deciding against candidates who showed photos of themselves doing a "kegstand" (headstand while drinking from a keg).

Everyone has the right to freedom of expression. But employers also have the right to decide against hiring someone because they believe that candidate has questionable judgment.

It's very difficult to decide who to hire for a job. Employers have very little to go on—usually a resume and a 15 to 30-minute job interview. Making hiring mistakes is costly. My message to students now is that whether or not you think it's fair, employers will Google you or look you up on these websites and similar ones in an effort to find out who you *really* are when you're not on your best behavior.

When you put questionable material on a website—or if you have a friend who posts objectionable photos, text, or music on a website connected to you with or without your approval—you might be affecting how professionals judge you. If that works against you, don't point fingers at anyone else.

CHAPTER TWO

Stay Positive

For one stretch during the early 1990s, I worked for a small business that developed training materials for companies in the pharmaceutical industry. It was a challenging job that often tested one's ability to stay positive.

I remember taking a total of four flights round-trip in order to attend a meeting that lasted all of 37 minutes at one client's headquarters. And all but a handful of those 37 minutes were devoted to hearing a Marketing manager lambaste his counterpart in Sales Training. She had made the unforgivable mistake of asking why my company had been brought in to handle an assignment instead of allowing it to be done internally. He stood up and made a scorecard assessing my company's successes versus those of Sales Training on previous projects.

The tally was 4-0 when she conceded the point. After coming a good distance to be there, I had sit through a tantrum.

On another occasion, I had to sit through an all-day meeting in which representatives of Marketing, Sales Training, Medical, and

Regulatory had to reach consensus on what our training materials would say. When we spent a half-hour debating what would be on the copyright page, I could see we were in for a long day. When it came to content, Marketing wanted to cast the information in the most favorable light for selling, while Medical wanted to be as balanced as possible about any drug's benefits and adverse effects. Sales Training wanted to make sure that everything was readily understandable. However, Regulatory's goal was to use legalese that would limit the company's potential liability, and that seemed to contradict the goal of making the material readable.

After surviving many such experiences, I successfully cultivated a reputation as someone who could clean up messy situations and drive projects through to conclusions. On several occasions, I inherited projects that teetered on the brink of disaster and had to make sure they reached completion without obliterating our relationship with the customer.

Odd as it may sound, I came to relish these challenges. Going into my critical first meeting with difficult and disillusioned customers, I always felt that there was little to lose. These customers had come to have a low opinion of our company: The worst I could do would be to prove that this perception was accurate. With such low expectations, I believed that if I merely proved to be a reasonable guy and kept us on task, then I would turn out to be better than they hoped.

The key was to stay positive and assume the best—even when there were valid reasons to have a more negative outlook.

We had one particularly difficult customer. They were renowned for their obsessive-compulsive attention to detail, bordering on the absurd at times. When engaged in medical writing, you expect to have to cite sources for key facts, but this company had driven one of our writers nuts by insisting on a source for virtually every sentence. "I swear, you can't even write something like

'Cancer is bad' without having them demand our source for such a statement," fumed one of my colleagues.

After umpteen requests for such citations, our writer lost it and blew up, and the client was furious. That was when I got the call to intervene. I had a phone conference with two people from the client who had complained bitterly about our writer. "I know that there have been some difficulties on this project," I said. "But rather than dissect that whole situation, I'd prefer to focus on identifying how we can work together to get what we both want—all your deliverables finished as efficiently and effectively as possible. By doing so, I think we can generate a lot more light than heat in our relationship."

To be honest, what I had heard about this client led me to think that they were a bit sadistic and ridiculous in their requests. But I concluded that there was little to be gained by questioning their motives or pinpointing whether the tensions between our organizations were really more our fault or theirs. Did it really matter anymore? We needed to move forward and stop wasting energy on finger-pointing.

The project proved to be extremely easy to complete. There was a sense of starting with a clean slate for both parties, and together we laid out all the tasks that needed be done and prioritized them. After my initial comments, we didn't allude any further to what had gone wrong; it was full speed ahead on the project.

The lesson I learned from that client was that you can't always help having internal doubts or concerns about a business partner or a colleague. However, you have to try to assume the best of people. When you stay positive, you can take a seemingly bad situation and turn it around. But when your actions reflect a negative outlook, you can take an ambiguous situation and turn it into something that truly is a bad situation!

The Second Key – Stay Positive

The second key to professional success is to stay positive. Former U.S. president Harry S Truman once said:

"A pessimist is one who makes difficulties of his opportunities and an optimist is one who makes opportunities of his difficulties."

Another president—Abraham Lincoln—had an analogous quote:

"People are about as happy as they make up their minds to be."

I have met several people who have married and then divorced for a variety of reasons. It can be very interesting to see the variety of perspectives that these individuals come to have about marriage. I have some divorced friends who actually asked me a lot of questions about my marriage—even asking to see my wedding video! The spirit of their attitude toward it seemed to be one of trying to see what could be learned by hearing about a successful and lasting marriage.

Conversely, I know of people who divorced and then seemingly gave up on marriage as a cursed institution. One family friend didn't even come to our wedding because she was so embittered about her own failed marriage. It somehow had ruined the concept altogether for her.

We all experience failures and disappointments in our professional and personal lives. That's nothing special. The question is whether we are able to learn from our mistakes, overcome our frustrations, and persist through adversity without souring on love, friendship, and careers. How we answer that question makes all the difference between a momentary stumble or a terminal flop.

Elements of Staying Positive

In analyzing many stories that had themes related to staying positive, I noticed many elements that comprise this key to professional success:

1. Assume the best.

If you've ever had a teacher, parent, or supervisor assume the best of you—even when you didn't particularly deserve it—you know how motivational it can be. In psychological terms, this is referred to as the Pygmalion Effect or the Rosenthal Effect. A study by Rosenthal and Jacobson (1968, 1992) showed that schoolteachers who expect great performance are far more likely to get it from their students compared to those who lack such expectations. In fact, students treated that way improved twice as much in performance than their peers who were not treated with this expectation.

Of course, the opposite is true, too: People tend to "live down" to poor expectations as well. So what's the significance for an aspiring professional? The more you expect the best out of yourself and your peers and supervisors, the more likely it is to lead to more positive outcomes for all involved. If you treat your supervisor as if she is terrific, she actually may become a better supervisor. If you treat your job as if it's critically important to the organization's success—whether or not it really is—you're going to perform better as well.

This is particularly important when you're dealing with ambiguity in the workplace. Your supervisor may be too busy to give you feedback, or it may be difficult to tell if you're doing well or not. The very worst thing you can do is to assume the worst and start decreasing your effort and effectiveness. By doing that, you can turn a pretty good or neutral situation into a bad one in a hurry.

2. Almost nothing is permanent in life.
Whatever your situation may be in life, it's going to change. When you're struggling through a difficult job search or unhappy with a job, it can have an incredible impact on your mood and outlook outside of those situations as well. It's basically impossible to stay positive every day of your life. But as much as you can, you have to remind yourself that difficult times don't last, and displaying a positive attitude can turn around tough situations quickly more often than you might imagine.

Sometimes you get hired into a job where people are skeptical about you from day one. In other situations, people assume that you're fantastic before you've even done anything. Either way, it's all subject to change. So don't dwell on the negatives of today, but don't forgot that a good situation doesn't always last, either. Do your best to stay positive amidst the inevitable ups and downs.

3. Understand the domino effect.
Success or failure in a job seldom boils down to just one shining or disastrous moment. Usually it's an accumulation of small successes—or problems—that gain momentum, like a snowball growing as it goes downhill.

For the majority of young professionals whom I have known, this works out positively: You show up early every day, and people start believing you're motivated—whether you really are or not. When they believe you're motivated, they may start giving you more interesting and challenging work to do. When you get more interesting work, it's even easier to be motivated, and you exceed expectations. It's a domino effect in which the situation just keeps getting better.

It goes the other way sometimes, too. For whatever reason, you have trouble getting to work on time, so people start assuming that you're not that excited about the job. Or you're given a low-level task, and you feel insulted so you do a crummy job on it. In both instances, it leads to more negative perceptions, fairly or unfairly. Maybe you start getting *worse* assignments, while the more exciting work goes to someone who shows they are able and willing to do it well. Either way, it's difficult to stop the momentum of the domino effect—especially if it's going in a negative direction.

4. Consider the consequences of all of your actions before acting.
When you're not happy in a job situation—when you're treated poorly by a co-worker or a supervisor, or when you have gone on a ton of interviews without a single offer—it becomes very tempting to let off steam. Sure, you could tell off your boss or quit a job in a huff. You could make some cutting, sarcastic comment to a co-worker, or start going through the motions when it's your tenth interview in three weeks.

But think before you actually do any of those things. Vent your frustrations to a friend or family member or career professional outside of work. Finding someone who can be objective may be helpful. Telling someone off may give you a few seconds or minutes of satisfaction, but it also may come back to haunt you for a long, long time after that satisfied feeling has evaporated.

Address problems or concerns by assuming the best of others and by putting the emphasis on finding solutions rather than focusing on blame. As the following stories illustrate, staying positive can lead to many unexpected rewards... but they may not be obvious ones until you're looking at the adversity from the rearview mirror.

True Stories about Staying Positive

The Closet Office

My co-op colleague Elizabeth Chilvers—who likes to say that she has been in this field since there were dinosaurs on Huntington

Avenue—told me this one. Years before I came to Northeastern, the university had hired a new employee but had no legitimate office to put him in. They gave him a tiny, windowless room that was scarcely bigger than a closet. It was so small that he had to keep the door open whenever he was there to avoid total claustrophobia; the only place for his desk was just barely inside the door. Even worse, he was in a busy corridor: It was just about impossible for people not to say hi to him as they walked by—he was just *right there.*

The situation stayed that way for some time. Inevitably, passers-by would not only say hello, they would express their amazement that anyone would have to work with such an odd arrangement. "This is horrible!" people would say.

The new hire didn't look at it that way. Sure, it was unusual, but he ended up meeting dozens of people in the first weeks on the job, and those people were immediately sympathetic to him. Better still, the traffic through the corridor often included some powerful decision-makers at the university back then, including the Provost and President. He developed many great connections directly because of his dubious location.

Another employee might have viewed the situation as an indignity. But, like all good employees, this guy found the opportunity amidst the challenge. His terrible office situation ended up being the first step in a long and productive career at the university.

"Everything I Didn't Expect"

At Drexel University, prospective co-op students go through three rounds of referrals—an A round, B round, and C round. When Anthony Caines—a student working toward joint Bachelor's and Master's degrees in 2008—went through that referral process the first time, he came very close to striking out altogether.

Competing against many more experienced candidates in the

A round, Anthony received only three interview requests out of 20 resume referrals. "And two of the three jobs were unpaid positions," Anthony recalls. "I was told that it was 'not terrible but not good' for a sophomore."

Anthony found himself wishing that the school would set aside positions that were only for first-time co-ops with no job experience. Of course, that's not the way companies do business in the real world, nor is it a typical practice at any co-op schools that I know.

For the B round, Anthony managed to get seven interviews from his 20 referrals. Again, though, some were unpaid. "I couldn't afford that," he says. Still, at least he had some interviews, and he felt that they all went well. But he wasn't getting any offers from employers with paid positions.

"I started thinking that I wasn't going to get a job," he says. "It's hard when you have no experience and you're competing against people who do have experience." As the C round approached, a sense of desperation kicked in. "I thought that maybe I should just accept a job, even it paid 25 cents an hour."

He also tried to figure out why he wasn't getting offers. "I'm the classic Italian kid from South Philadelphia," he said. "And that's obvious from how I talk. So I thought maybe it was just that other candidates seemed—I don't know—more refined in their communication skills. Plus, when I'm in a suit, I look like an extra from *The Sopranos*."

Anthony decided that multiple practice interviews might help. He worked on his verbal communication skills with his co-op coordinator Rita Crane among others. "I don't even notice my accent," Anthony says. "So I had to work on that. As you can tell, I also talk really fast. And I talk with my hands all the time. It can be really distracting."

Building awareness about his communication style, Anthony felt more prepared for the C round. He got nine or ten interviews from his 20 resume referrals that time. Interviewing for a merchandising job in the main corporate office of a chain of retail stores targeting teens and "tweens," Anthony faced a tough interview with a poker-faced woman... but he got the job. "I was shocked to get an offer after going 0 for 15," he said. Apparently the employer just thought he seemed more interested than other candidates.

Initially it was a "go-fer" job. Anthony made copies and nametags, handling mundane administrative tasks for the company. But after a brutally tough job search, "I was just happy to do anything." That carried him through the first three weeks, though he admitted that soon "it became tough; I need responsibility."

A lucky break then occurred. The Assistant Buyer quit, and the stores were swamped. Due to his high energy over those critical first three weeks, "I was thrown right into the fire. Suddenly I was working 50 hours a week—more than any other co-op. I was calling vendors, placing orders, you name it."

There were many lessons taken from that first job search and the position itself. "It was everything I didn't expect," Anthony says. "I learned that you need to keep your head up. During my search, it got to the point where I didn't want to go out. I was so depressed with rejection after rejection."

Without a paying job, Anthony says he may have had to transfer out of Drexel. On the brink of a complete failure, though, he had managed to stay positive enough to keep fine-tuning his interviewing skills and to have faith enough to show more interest in a job than the next guy. As so often happens, that energy transferred over into his approach to the job. Anthony showed that you need to seize opportunities, as they don't come along every day.

The Power of Negative Thinking

"Steve Padgett" had a great first co-op, working at Boston Beer Company. When it came time to interview for his next co-op, Steve interviewed with one of my best employers. It was definitely a "reach" job for him, and he didn't get it. But he made a great impression on the interviewers, who told me that they definitely wanted to see him on the interview schedule for his third and last co-op. With a little more experience, they thought he would be great.

So Steve went to Gillette and did a great job. Around the same time, though, he became involved with a young woman from Baltimore. He decided that he would try to find his own job around Baltimore for his third co-op—that way he could be closer to her.

He went down to Baltimore in early September to try to line up a job for January. Unfortunately, it was September 2001. The job market in his field wasn't great, and when 9/11 happened, hiring basically ground to a halt for an extended time. He did have several interviews but met with nothing but rejection.

I was not worried. After all, I knew that this top employer would be back on campus, and they were already predisposed to hire Steve. Sure, it wasn't in Baltimore, but it would be a fantastic job. Steve agreed to interview with them again.

What a surprise and disappointment it was for me when I got the feedback from the employer after the interviews. They could not figure out what had happened to the promising, enthusiastic job seeker of a year ago. He seemed uninterested and negative in the interview.

I was perplexed but assumed that maybe his heart just wasn't in a job that was so far away from Baltimore. When I met with him, though, he assured me that he definitely wanted the job and was disappointed that it didn't work out.

Eventually we pieced together what had happened. After repeatedly encountering rejection while interviewing in Baltimore, Steve gradually became more and more pessimistic about getting hired. So he went into the interview thinking, "Well, here we go again... Another interview, another time for my hopes to get dashed..." and he proceeded to go through the motions in his preparation and execution for the interview.

"You know what you remind me of?" I told him. "You're like a guy who has a really painful break-up with someone and who then goes on a first date with someone else a few months later. And he goes on that date still feeling angry and bitter toward that old girlfriend.

"But you know what? The woman he's dating now, she doesn't represent the problem. In fact, she's a possible SOLUTION to that problem! But he'll never find out, because she's going to conclude that he's simply an angry and bitter guy as opposed to an upbeat and positive person."

Steve got the message, big time. It was a tough lesson, as a great opportunity had eluded him. But he completely turned his attitude around and got another excellent job. More importantly, he learned that whatever adversity you encounter, you need to learn what you can from it and then move on.

The Vicious Circle

Several years ago, I visited two co-ops who had been in a new job for about a month. When I met with them, they basically attacked me verbally. "This should NOT be a job for co-op students," one of them said. "There's nothing to do; we aren't learning anything."

"The tasks that we're given to do are insulting!" the other said. "And that's when there IS something to do, which is only a few hours a day." I didn't appreciate their accusatory tone, but I bit my lip. Although many other students had worked in the job before without incident, it was always possible that things had changed. Maybe now there was just nothing to do but busywork.

Afterwards, I met with the manager of the two disgruntled employees. I opted for a neutral, open-ended question: "So, how's it going with your two co-ops?" Imagine my surprise when the manager heaved a deep sigh, looked me in the eye, and said, "We wish we could get these two to DO SOMETHING."

It appeared to be a contradiction. For a moment, I thought, "Well, this might be the easiest problem to solve in the history of cooperative education!" Of course, it was not nearly that simple.

Without anyone intending it, a vicious circle had emerged. Like many employers, this supervisor had given the two new workers a few extremely simple tasks on their first few days of work. This is not uncommon. It's not that most employers assume that you're an idiot until you prove otherwise; rather, they want to let you ease your way into the pool instead of throwing you in the deep end to see if you'll sink or swim.

Almost always, a new hire recognizes this and does that simple task efficiently and effectively. Quite often, our co-ops exceed expectations in the process and quickly show that they deserve more advanced work. In this case, however, the two co-ops not only perceived the task to be insulting: They responded by doing a poor job and by taking twice as long as anticipated to complete it.

Neither the workers nor the manager did a great job in communicating about what had happened or why. So the manager basically assumed that his two new hires were not very capable employees, and he responded by giving them something even more mundane to do! Naturally, my unhappy pair were even more offended and continued to express that in their attitude and performance.

By the time this came to light when I visited, both the supervisor and the employees were entrenched in their negative perceptions about each other. For the next few months, I tried to see if we could turn around the situation. Ultimately, one student quit the job early and the other was fired for ongoing attendance and attitude problems: Neither received a passing grade for co-op.

With all of this going on, I talked to four or five previous co-ops who had been in the job. All said that it was a good first co-op job. Yes, there was downtime, but then again if you showed some interest and initiative, there were opportunities to learn a great deal about networking and building web pages when it was slow. All of the previous co-ops had emerged from the job with better computer skills and a terrific reference. It all started with assuming the best of the employer and the job.

Meanwhile, the two co-ops who had problems continued to have them. One had ongoing squabbles with people at NU. When the other one graduated, he very much wanted a job with the federal government. As part of the process, a government contractor came to my office to ask me questions about this student as a candidate. As you might imagine, I told him I would have to decline comment on the individual and recommended that he contact the candidate's previous employers to see what they would say about him. I can only imagine how *that* went!

A Supposedly Bad Job

Years ago, a local beer distributor used to hire co-op students through me. Basically the job entailed going around to liquor stores and making sure that all the product available was as fresh as it needed to be. I never thought it was all that great of a job, but they would hire people with *no* experience and give them a *little*, at least.

I had one co-op get fired from that job, maybe two. One guy just could not get to work on time and eventually was let go. He insisted that it was a terrible job and that no one could blame him for being unmotivated. Obviously, getting fired seldom reflects well on anyone, but I had a hard time disagreeing with his assertion that there was little if anything to learn in that job.

And then "Peter Schaeffer" took the job. Born in Germany, Peter's English wasn't fantastic, and he had no work experience in this country. But Peter was one of these people who was just happy to be alive. Every time he came in to my office, it was with a huge smile and all kinds of positive energy: "Scott!! How's it going?! I'm doing GREAT!"

After getting hired by that beer distributor, Peter went into the office every day with that energy. He was always happy to come in: "Hey, I'm German: We *love* beer!" he would say, much to everyone's amusement. And he would ask questions reflecting considerable intellectual curiosity: "What kind of database are you using to keep track of the returns?" "Why don't we have a better system of anticipating when product is low?"

Within two weeks, his manager called him to his office. "Tomorrow I want you to leave your uniform at home: Wear a suit. Anybody can do what you're doing. We want you to work on our database as a sales analyst."

All of a sudden a hopelessly "bad job" turned into a very good one indeed. The bonus for me was that I became known as "the guy who gave me Peter Schaeffer's resume." What a win-win. It never would have happened if he didn't show that someone with his attitude and interest level deserved much more.

Late-Night E-Mails

In October 2005, my colleague Bill Munze asked me to pop down to his office to look at an e-mail sent to him by his student "Keefe Calladine." As we walked down, Bill asked me if I had had any troubles with Keefe.

"Not at all," I said. I had only met Keefe once. We talked about some jobs, and I put him on an interview schedule for one of my top employers—even though he was a "reach" candidate for that position.

Bill read Keefe's e-mail to me. If it were in a Harry Potter novel, you would have called it a "howler." It was a furious burst of writing: I could almost picture him banging away on a computer keyboard. There were all sorts of strange accusations in it: No one in co-op was helping him... He should have more interviews by now... And—much to my amazement—he told Bill that he was convinced that the only reason he didn't get the job with my top employer was that I had told that employer to hire "my" students instead of students who worked with other co-op faculty at Northeastern. It was an absolutely amazing accusation!

I took a deep breath. "Let me guess," I said to Bill. "Was this e-mail written at midnight?"

"Not quite," Bill said. "You're off by about 40 minutes."

You see, this unpleasant phenomenon rears its ugly head periodically when we work with students. At the end of a long and perhaps frustrating day, some people check their e-mail and maybe find that they didn't get a job... or that someone else did get that job. And it's terribly simple—as well as simply terrible—to bash out an e-mail to vent one's frustration.

The only problem is that once you send an e-mail out, you can't take it back. And when you've said something nasty in writing—something you surely *never* would have said in a face-to-face conversation—it sure is awkward to have to face the consequences.

Bill invited Keefe in to discuss his concerns with the two of us. As you might imagine, he was quite sheepish when asked to explain why he felt justified in accusing me of engaging in highly unprofessional behavior. He muttered that he heard that the employer had offered a job to a guy he knew—a guy who Keefe did not believe to be a strong candidate. Somehow he concluded that the only way this could have happened would be if I had intervened.

I reminded him about our previous conversation—I had told him that he was a definite long-shot hire for this position. As it turned out, the interviewer told me that Keefe basically had bombed the interview. And now Keefe wanted to blame someone for that.

On the whole, Keefe was pretty embarrassed by the end of that conversation. But I think he learned that you should never send an e-mail or leave a voice mail while you're in a foul mood and that it's not advisable to assume the worst of others when things go wrong.

The Interrupted Interview Schedule

My co-op colleague Mary Rose Tichar at Case Western Reserve University offers this story about a student who never let his performance waver on his first co-op, even after he realized he was in the wrong type of company. As she describes below, it took just one 20-minute interview for his perseverance to pay off on his next job search.

The most important thing that electrical engineering student "Nigel Dewey" learned on his first co-op was what he does *not* want to do for a career. He ruled out becoming a programmer and found that he is more interested in hardware and analog or mixed signal integrated circuit design. His employer didn't offer any opportunities for him to achieve those goals. Fortunately, he never lost sight of everything that *could* be gained from that job. He learned how and when to speak up. He became more confident, especially when it came to his communication skills.

By the time he came back on campus, I knew that he was going to go places in his career. Although there weren't any fireworks to report about Nigel's co-op, his diligence, attention to detail, and thoroughness with everything he does created a very fun scenario in my office when the time came for his second job search. Once resumes were sent out, Nigel's name appeared on *every* electrical engineering interview schedule. One of the first companies on campus that semester was Intel. Nigel was the first interview on the schedule – 8:45. At 9:05, the interviewer came into my office and said, "Can I please use your phone? I need to call corporate and get permission to hire this student right away."

Nigel was the first of 13 students on the schedule, but obviously made such an incredible impression in 20 minutes that an offer was made within the half-hour. I will never forget the employer's enthusiasm in his quest to make Nigel an immediate offer.

Not The "Friends And Family Program"

These days Amy Black, Northeastern University Class of 2000, is a successful professional at a Fortune 500 company in New Jersey. Recently, though, she reflected back to her very first professional job search, when she looked for her first co-op job as a marketing concentrator at Northeastern.

Amy was a student-athlete, competing on our Varsity Swimming team. So on top of having little job experience at the time, she had to find an employer who could accommodate her work schedule limitations. Every morning, practice ended at 8 a.m., making it challenging to get to work any earlier than 9. And then she would have to leave work by 4 p.m. for 5:00 practice. On top of that, there were meets that would make it impossible for her to work on a number of Fridays.

Her co-op coordinator sent her resume to about 20 employers, leading to a dozen interviews, all of which ended in rejection. Having the option of choosing between candidates who were available for 40 hours per week, employers found Amy's situation too complicated. Why deal with that if you don't have to?

Her coordinator told her to give up, convinced that it wasn't going to happen for Amy. Instead, she cast her net more broadly and started looking at our accounting jobs. She found a position with Ernst and Young and interviewed with them just a few weeks before the scheduled start date. They were willing to be flexible and hired her.

Amy told me that she looks back at this experience as one of the most powerful lessons she received. "I remember calling my mom, really upset, and saying 'Why doesn't anyone want to hire me?' And my mom said, 'That's why you're at Northeastern.' When I graduated, my friends at other schools were looking for their first real jobs, and they were freaking out. They had what I call the 'Friends and Family Program.' They got internships through connections that they had through people they knew; they never had to compete for jobs."

Amy identified a few "takeaways" from this tough experience. "First, never give up! You need to learn to be able to handle rejection. Second, the most competitive part of Northeastern is getting a job, not getting grades. And now in my job searches people really do react to those great jobs that I had."

Imaginary Crisis

For many young professionals, it's very common to worry about what it means when a co-worker or supervisor is grumpy, distracted, or in a foul mood. If you're conscientious, it's easy to believe that you might be responsible for that behavior. But you have to be careful to not jump to conclusions.

In September 2005, I received an e-mail from "Natalie Hartwick," one of my general management students. She was two and a half months into her first six-month co-op job, and it seemed like everything was going wrong. She was almost positive that her supervisor was unhappy with her.

We exchanged several e-mails and phone calls about it, as I tried to figure out what was going on. Natalie's boss had barely talked to her for several weeks, and she was kind of abrupt when they did talk. Natalie had been given no feedback as to how she had performed thus far, and she didn't feel like it was a good time to push for that. The group was facing a deadline on a major deliverable, and she didn't think that her boss would want to take time to discuss a co-op's concerns for the time being. Perhaps that could happen in three weeks or so, when the project was completed.

Natalie really wanted me to tell her that everything was fine and that there was no reason for her to be concerned. Of course, I didn't know that. But the biggest theme of our conversations was that Natalie needed to do everything in her power to not let the uncertainty affect her attitude or performance. My greatest fear was that Natalie would start *acting like a poor employee* just because she believed that this was how her supervisor looked at her.

"Whatever she thinks of you, that would be a disaster!" I told her. "It would either confirm and strengthen a negative opinion that she already holds... or it could even give her that negative opinion for the first time." I had to concede that her supervisor *might* be unhappy with her—I couldn't reassure her on that front—but there were many other explanations as well. There was legitimate reason to believe that her boss might be stressed out due to the deadline and that Natalie was a low priority for the time being.

A few weeks later Natalie sent me a jubilant e-mail. She had handled it perfectly, keeping quiet and getting her work done efficiently until the group hit their deliverable target—even finding others who could help her on tasks so she wouldn't have to distract her boss. When the time was right, she requested a meeting with her supervisor and didn't say anything about her worst fears. She just said that she'd love to have feedback on her performance so she could make any necessary adjustments to ensure the best possible performance evaluation at the end of her work term.

The evaluation was outstanding. The supervisor was apologetic about her lack of time to mentor Natalie, and she expressed appreciation about how Natalie had persevered despite a lot of stress and uncertainty. Natalie learned a great lesson about assuming the best in an ambiguous situation, at a time when a more pessimistic outlook could have changed everything for the worse.

CHAPTER THREE

Exceed Expectations

One legendary story from my family's history stretches back to The Great Depression. My grandfather, Peter Cushnie, was a well-educated man for his era, a Scottish immigrant with a college degree. But when the economy tanked in the 1930s, he lost his well-paid position at an engineering firm and needed to pound the pavement in search for work.

Given the circumstances, the best job he was able to obtain was a lowly position in a grocery store. They hired him to bag groceries. Sometimes I try to imagine myself in his shoes: If I were reduced to doing menial work as a full-time job, I think it would be a humbling and depressing development. How motivated would I be?

This was not an issue for my grandfather. One of my mother's earliest memories is the night before he began his new job. He didn't sit around bemoaning his fate. Instead he had the family take all of their groceries out of the cabinets and refrigerator—a new enough appliance that the family still was in the habit of calling it the "icebox." The goods were laid out in a carefully disorganized pile on the dining room table. My grandfather practiced bagging them as fast as he could.

This was harder than anyone under the age of 75 might imagine. My grandfather had this job shortly before grocery bags became widespread in use. Some customers had their own bags, but most needed to have their groceries tied into a parcel. The "bagger" needed to pull the right length of paper off of a spool, ripping it off on the metal teeth attached to the spool holder. Then the bagger placed the right amount of groceries on top of the paper before folding the paper around over the goods and securing it with string.

After many attempts, my grandfather managed to get the job done quickly without wasting paper. Obsessed with making the most of an opportunity to provide for his family during a difficult time, he set out to exceed expectations from day one.

He did just that. Soon the store promoted him to a manager's position in the produce department. My grandfather was a fastidious man, and he despaired of ever getting his hands clean after a day of handling fruits and vegetables. But the role gave him a pay increase and the opportunity to bring home food items that had been damaged or overripe. He continued to put everything he had into the job, proving to be an incredibly hard worker who would protect the store's interests at all times.

By the time the Depression ended, the grocery store chain offered him his own store to manage. After mulling it over, he and my grandmother decided it would be best for him to resume his career as an engineering draftsman. He proved to be such a dedicated employee in that role that they waived the usual retirement age of 65. He continued working until age 78. He died in 1985 at the age of 85. Amazingly, my grandmother lived until the age of 102, dying in 2006. Due to the fact that he had worked so long and managed his money with legendary Scottish thrift, she was completely and generously provided for throughout those 20-plus years.

So when I work with college students who have come into our co-op program with no college degree and no professional experience, I hope that if nothing else they can begin their first professional job with a drive to exceed expectations. Hearing that story about my grandfather repeatedly throughout my childhood, I may lack patience when occasionally a first-time co-op student tells me it is "beneath him" (or her) to have to do data entry or filing.

Obviously it's important to try to get the best job you can get, whether you're looking for an internship or the final job of your career. Once you accept ANY job, though, you need to do everything you can to exceed expectations in whatever you are asked to do. As the stories in this chapter will show, going the extra mile in a job very often leads to unexpected possibilities.

The Third Key – Exceed Expectations

The third key to professional success is to exceed expectations. Author Robert Louis Stevenson said:

"Don't judge each day by the harvest you reap, but by the seeds you plant."

Dale Carnegie—a renowned public speaker and author of *How To Win Friends And Influence People*—said:

"Most of the important things in the world have been accomplished by people who kept trying when there seemed to be no hope at all."

On a more humorous note, there is also Woody Allen's famous (and frequently misquoted) line that "80 percent of success is just showing up." Really, though, the first step toward exceeding expectations as a professional is just getting to work on time and energized. It's quite different from the classroom. You need to be rested and ready to be sharp and driven for eight full hours, not just for an hour or two at a time.

After that, there are many sources that might inspire you to go beyond merely showing up. For some, it's a sense of competitive drive—wanting to be better than others. For others, it's more a matter of pride and character that fuels that commitment to go the extra mile. It even may be a less noble desire: A person just might recognize that being great at what they do is in their selfish best interest.

When I ask first-time co-ops why it's important to do well in their forthcoming jobs, most of them realize that excellent job performance will give them better references, an improved resume, and possible future career opportunities with that employer. Yet surprisingly few recognize that great job performance often directly leads to improving your actual job responsibilities—and sometimes that happens in a matter of days and weeks. That's the most fascinating payoff of exceeding expectations.

Elements of Exceeding Expectations

In collecting stories featuring themes related to exceeding expectations, I came up with several elements that comprise this key to professional success:

1. Go above and beyond.
As you'll see, sometimes it's a very small choice that paves the way for much greater opportunities: It might be volunteering for an unpopular project or to stay late. It could be showing extra enthusiasm right at the time when a manager needs someone to step up. But it's clear that those who achieve great success in their careers were individuals who were not content to do their assigned job pretty well and leave it at that. They were employees

who made sure that they did a great job on their assigned duties and then showed that they were hungry for bigger challenges.

2. Outwork others: Persistence often beats out talent.
Some of the most inspiring success stories that I've collected concerned people who had very little going for them at the start of their careers: poor grades, mediocre language skills, negligible job experience, and so forth. For those who overcome those hurdles, much of it boils down to their willingness to outwork their peers. I can't count how many times in my career where I've seen a job candidate go into the interview process as an unbelievable long shot on paper and yet beat out someone who was more intelligent and experienced. It usually happens through sheer effort.

Boston University hockey coach Jack Parker has a great goal for his team for each game. He wants them to *deserve* to win. Sometimes you don't win in sports or in your career. Maybe someone has more ability and talent than you do, and they have a work ethic to match it. But whenever you don't get a job—or a promotion, or the best raise—you want to be able to look back and be satisfied with your effort, regardless of the outcome.

3. It's fun to do things well.
When you're working full-time hours, you're spending the most significant part of five days per week in your work environment. The more you immerse yourself in it and try to master it, the more you're going to enjoy those long hours. Almost anything a business might do has the potential to be interesting—but sometimes only if you ask enough questions and dig deeply enough into the subject matter to find out what it takes to do it as well as possible.

Sometimes I tell my students, "The more you learn about a subject, the more you realize how little you know about it... and how much more there is to learn." On top of that, it's a great feeling to be recognized as one of the best in your field. You can have a terrific time by becoming an expert in your field and learning how to wow your supervisor, colleagues, and customers.

4. Don't get distracted from the goal.
In most work environments, there are many distractions that can lead you off course and prevent you from the goal of exceeding expectations. Often there are organizational politics, and it's easy to get your energy sucked away from your job by the rumors, gossip, and power plays that may be going on around you. Being aware of politics can be important, but developing an obsession with them can distract you from performing as well as you can.

Likewise, most organizations have their complainers, cynics, and malingerers—people who will delight in converting you to their agenda of finger-pointing and finding ways to do as little as possible. Be wary of those who try to convince you that it's somehow in your best interest to fail to meet expectations.

Lastly, there are plenty of temptations that can affect individuals without any assistance from those around them. For many, the primary temptation is technology. People may or may not figure it out if you're on your cellphone, the Internet, or your BlackBerry... but whether or not they know that you're distracting yourself with technology, they definitely will notice your lack of productivity.

5. There are no rewards or bonuses for just showing up at work.
If you're a member of the Millennial Generation—born around 1982 or later—you may have grown up in a culture that rewarded *participation* instead of *excellence.* In some ways, this is very nice: Everyone who plays soccer or is on a swim team comes home with a ribbon or trophy, and each participant feels good about himself or herself. Competition is downplayed in favor of teamwork; some individuals go through their first 18 years without having to handle much criticism.

Although that's very nice, it's not what most professional

environments are like. You won't often get the same raise as everyone else just because you were on the same team. Many people apply for a job or promotion, but sometimes only one gets it.

In short, it's good to remember that your career advancement will depend on how well you demonstrate your ability to outwork others as well as set ambitious targets and hit them. Adapting to a competitive workplace depends on your ability to recognize that you no longer get rewards for just living, breathing, and showing up.

Woody Allen did say that 80 percent of success was just showing up. Even if that figure were accurate, an 80 percent in the classroom equates to a B-. So let's see what it takes to get an A+ as a professional.

True Stories about Exceeding Expectations

The Last Shall Be First

In my early years at Northeastern University, the job market for Management Information Systems was bountiful for our students. The demand outstripped the supply, and by the time the work term officially started, I only had one student left to place: "Eddie Huang."

It wasn't as if he hadn't put in the effort. Born in China and first exposed to the English language at age 15, his communication skills were a perpetual deal-breaker in his interviews. His biggest asset was that he was a wonderful guy. He was concerned but always came to my office with a smile on his face, hungry for any advice I could give him. In the weeks counting down toward co-op, he literally went on at least ten interviews, and the story was always the same—nice guy, but we don't think he'll be able to communicate with our other employees.

Finally he had the dubious distinction of being the sole survivor among the ranks of the unemployed. A new job came in, and I sent out his resume, period. The employer interviewed him and followed up to see if I had other candidates. Learning that I did not, the employer hired Eddie.

I heard nothing for the next six weeks and then went out to visit that employer. As soon as I sat down, the manager said, "You know, I only hired this guy because he was the only candidate you had left..."

He paused, and I tensed up. Here it comes, I thought. This guy isn't working out; no one understands him... We're letting him go. As I held my breath, the manager completed the sentence. "...and it's the luckiest thing that's ever happened to me as a manager." Apparently Eddie was just a ray of sunshine in that job. He did any task with a smile, did it perfectly, and came back eager for more. He loved the job, and they loved him. And they said he had a great sense of humor! This seemed strange to me, but I didn't question it.

After that co-op, Eddie came back to classes and told me he wanted to return to that employer. After all, he was happy. I took a deep breath—knowing that we would be in for another difficult job search—and explained to him that the job was an entry-level job, and it was time for him to move on to a greater challenge. He heard me out and then agreed that it was the right thing to do, although neither of us relished another lengthy round of interviews.

The first job helped him get more interviews, but the interviewers raised the same questions and doubts. After many failures, one manager called to say that it was down to Eddie and another candidate, but that she thought she was going to go with the other candidate because of the communication issue. Although I rarely intervene with such decisions, I told her, "That's fine. Just do me a favor: Before you make a final decision, call Eddie's boss from his first co-op. Whatever you decide after that is fine with me."

Naturally, she offered the job to Eddie. I visited him again on the site and was pleased to see that he was still utilizing one of my early suggestions: He kept a notebook to write down any English words he didn't understand and to make sure he didn't have to go back to his supervisor more often than necessary when completing tasks.

They invited me to attend their group IT meeting, and Eddie promptly took out his notebook. "Oh, Eddie," his manager teased, "You know that nothing important happens at these meetings... Why are you always writing things down?"

Eddie didn't miss a beat. "Only have four megabytes RAM up here," he said, tapping his head. "Must write down to remember more." The group cracked up with laughter. "Where did we get this guy?" someone said. Eddie was the life of the party and a model employee to boot.

Eddie did one more co-op with that employer, doing more advanced PC/LAN Support work. For his last co-op, he forged beyond his comfort zone once again and landed a completely different job—a database design position with a major software developer. He got an offer from that employer with a starting salary of $48,000—pretty good pay for the late 1990s. Before graduation, he won not only a Co-op Award for outstanding job performance but also the Pratt Award, which we give out each year to a student who displays outstanding personal and professional development throughout their years at Northeastern.

Whenever I have a student who works hard in the job search process and is one of the last to get a co-op job, I still think of Eddie. The troubles that students sometimes face in looking for a job certainly appear to be smaller when seen through the rearview mirror; a strong work ethic and positive attitude can overcome enormous obstacles and glaring weaknesses.

Changing Of The Guard

Aviad Benzikry was excited going into his first six-month co-op job. His only work experiences were as a lifeguard and a barista at a coffee chain, but now he had obtained a position at a Fortune 500 company in a corporate finance role.

However, the co-op he was replacing in the job did everything she could to deflate his expectations. "You will be SO bored in this job," she told him with obvious bitterness. It was her third and final co-op, and she had expected and hoped for more. Instead, she said that most of her days were spent filing.

Aviad shrugged it off. "Whatever," he thought. She struck him as jaded, and he didn't take her comments too seriously. "I was so excited to work at a big company," Aviad recalls. His work ethic and attitude reflected that, and before long his boss said, "You look like you really want to be here."

Like the previous co-op, Aviad started off doing filing and light accounts payable work. He soon discovered that the previous co-op had made many mistakes, and he set out to correct them all. It took a few months, but he corrected all of her errors and set up the systems to work much more smoothly. One customer—previously known as the worst customer in terms of accounts payable—ended up giving Aviad a gift to thank him for his efforts in straightening out their issues.

By then some opportunities emerged in the group. When a full-time female employee left on maternity leave, Aviad was given her responsibilities. Suddenly he wasn't filing any more. He was handling budgeting and managing all the accounts for one of the major finance groups. He took care of journal entries in an SAP database—and that had been his boss's job when Aviad was first hired!

"My attitude was 100 percent to go in there and be ready to learn—be a sponge," Aviad told me with one month to go on his first job. "I've had to learn everything from scratch—how to dress, how to approach people in their office, how to use the company's version of IM [Instant Messenger]... This is legitimately the greatest experience I've ever had."

When there is a "changing of the guard" from one worker to the next—or when you talk to other full-time employees soon after obtaining a job—it can be a valuable way to learn some inside information about the company, how to succeed, and what pitfalls exists. It's good to hear other people's perspectives, but you also have to make sure that you're not infected by someone else's negativity. If that had happened here, Aviad might have gone through six months of lightweight work and missed out on the most amazing opportunity of his career to date.

The Bagel Boy

Several years ago, I had one of the then Big Six accounting firms come on campus to interview Management Information Systems students for the first time. After getting a sense of what they were seeking, I set up an interview schedule for them and forwarded the candidates' resumes to the primary interviewer.

One of the hiring managers called back the day before the interviews occurred on campus. "For the most part the schedule looks great, but I think you made one mistake," he said. "You included one guy who clearly doesn't belong on the schedule. He has no experience."

"If you don't mind, I'd like to ask you to just trust me on that one," I said. He seemed surprised but agreed.

The candidate in question was Ron Ordell. A Washington State native, Ron had impressed me before he even got to Northeastern. He and his dad made a point of visiting my office when he was still a senior in high school, and he asked several sharp questions about what co-op would entail if he came to Boston.

Granted, Ron's first resume was not one that would stand out to an employer seeking seasoned individuals. As I recall, his two best jobs were working at a Baskin Robbins and a bagel shop. But he was a smart, driven, self-confident young man, and he really wowed me in his practice interview. He deserved a shot.

So the employer came on campus. Ron was maybe fifth on the interview schedule. After three or four interviews, the interviewers emerged and clearly were pleased. "We're really pleased with these candidates; they really know how to interview." They already had seen a couple plausible hires, and one of them commented that they had already done better than they had in two days at another university.

But after Ron interviewed with them, their enthusiasm had transformed into a state of shock. They were stunned by his interview. "I couldn't believe it," one interviewer said. "He literally gave us an economics lesson."

Several goals were fulfilled that day. My students had shown a new employer that Northeastern students needed to be taken very seriously in recruiting—even those that didn't look like much on paper. And Ron reminded me that an intelligent and driven person who is willing to outwork the competition will rise to the top in a hurry. He went back home to Microsoft for a subsequent co-op and recently took a great position at Nike. It's scary to imagine how well he might interview these days, now that he has much more than the bagel boy job on his resume.

Going The Extra Kilometer

When Sky-Lyn Priddle first began her collegiate career as a

Health Sciences major, she envisioned herself becoming a physician eventually. But given that she attends the University of Waterloo in Canada—the world's largest cooperative education program—it's not surprising that she has been exposed to a variety of opportunities that have led to some twists and turns in her career.

She experienced some literal twists and turns on her first co-op. Working as an Outdoor Education Intern for the Scarborough Outdoor Education School (SOES) in Ontario, she overcame the doubts that she had about whether she was cut out to be a teacher.

"I wasn't sure I wanted to teach; I didn't like public speaking," she told me. But she thought that a co-op would be a good opportunity to try it out. Given the nature of the job, she had to overcome her inexperience in chopping wood and starting fires. Then she had to teach cross-country skiing to sixth graders, despite the fact that her own Nordic ability was not exactly advanced. And she had to focus on extra effort instead of buying into the negative expectations that had been passed along by her colleagues.

"I got the slower group," Sky said. "The other teachers didn't like the slower group because they fell down more and made slow progress. I was a little nervous: What if a kid gave up? So I tried to think of games they could play."

For every hill the group navigated, she came up with a new question. "What's the name of your favorite candy bar? Scream it out as you go over the hill!"

To her surprise, she found she actually preferred to work with the group. "You get to interact more," she said.

One skier fell on every single hill. "He had a great attitude," Sky said. "I just kept saying 'You're getting better!' And I kept giving him tips." That boy—the very slowest of the slow—was very thankful at the end. "You're such a great skier; you should be in the Olympics," he told Sky.

"Every time now I would ask for the slower group," she said. "It really energizes me to go the extra mile when learning a new task."

By the end of her co-op, Sky's career path had proved to be as unpredictable as that cross-country trail. Now she definitely wants to be teacher. Her co-op taught her how education could be a satisfying career because of the relationships that she was great at developing with students—by going the extra kilometer, in this case.

Beyond Coffee And Photocopies

Several years after graduating from Northeastern, Chris Wright now works for a global bank; his role is with a group that specializes in making tax refund loans. He's quick to describe how the co-op experiences he obtained in college have been the foundation of his success ever since.

"It's funny, but when people I work with find out that I did co-ops and internships throughout college, they say, 'Oh, you were an intern? Were you making copies and getting coffee?'"

His co-workers have no idea to what degree his co-op experiences have proved to be the foundation for his subsequent professional success. "There's every kind of job you can imagine when you're an NU co-op," he says. "If you want a job that's more than making copies, they're there."

So how to did he manage to sort out the really worthwhile jobs from those that had less to offer? "From my experience, it seemed to be a willingness to go the extra mile. You need to study the jobs carefully and put time in to just go through the hundreds and hundreds of jobs," he says. "It's a great network. You can always find someone who worked at a company and find out what the job was *really* like."

One habit that he developed in those jobs that has stayed with him is being accountable for his results. "I kind of enjoy taking on the responsibility myself," he says. "I am given projects, and I run with them. I've built on my co-op experiences in doing that."

As an intern, he worked tons of hours for a sports marketing firm, and that level of commitment was taken for granted. Now the tables have turned. "That's the flip side of being used to crunch all those hours as an intern," he says of the extra hours he puts in now. At his current position, he has won two recognition awards, been promoted, and taken on a bigger role in marketing. "It's all about being able to organize and think on my own two feet."

That started with his co-op experiences. And he got better jobs than some students did because he sweated the details in the job search process.

The All-Time Best Interviewee

Of all the co-ops I've ever worked with, Dan Ely still ranks as the best interviewee of all time. Dan actually changed my mind about what was possible in interviewing, and some of his thoughts were counterintuitive at first glance. For one thing, Dan loved early-morning interviews—the earlier the better, in fact. "I figure that the interviewer might be half-awake, fumbling for his coffee, and meanwhile I'm going to come in with a ton of energy and wake him up!"

Dan went to the extreme of creating two different types of interview questions for the closing of the interview. He prepared conservative questions and more aggressive questions, and then waited to see how much rapport and how much of a comfort level he managed to create during the interview before determining whether he wanted to ask intense questions or more low-key ones. So in interviewing for a major oil company, he might ask something benign like "What would my typical day be like as a co-op here" if the interviewer seemed a bit distant. But if he felt that comfort level, he might ask "How is your organization preparing for the fact that fossil fuels may run out on this planet within the next several decades?"

Most impressive, though, was how Dan opened his interview. You see, Dan was partially paralyzed; he did not have full use of his legs. As a result, he needed metal crutches to walk, and he had a slow and somewhat awkward gait. So when he first walked in for his interview, he could sense the tension, anxiety, and—worst of all—distraction of the interviewer. And, of course, the interviewer would never be so rude as to ask Dan about what had happened to him.

So Dan would kick off the conversation by saying, "You're probably wondering why I'm on these crutches." He would proceed to explain how he had a motorbike accident a few years earlier and how that kept him from having fully functioning legs. "However, it doesn't keep me from being able to take a computer apart and put it back together again... The only way it affects me as an employee that I'm not incredibly fast in getting around the office."

Dan told me that once he had told the interviewer this, he or she would just relax and really focus on him, Dan, a person, as opposed to just some guy with some worrisome disability.

Dan didn't relish talking about his accident, but he also was a very competitive guy. The interview process was a game to him, and he was determined to come out on top. His open and honest communication and sensitivity to the discomfort of others did both parties a favor by humanizing him.

That goal accomplished, Dan could proceed to blow them away

with his interview strategy and those amazing questions. He got his last co-op at Microsoft and is still there many years later.

Into The Driver's Seat

For his second co-op, Drexel University marketing student Anthony Caines obtained a job in a commercial law firm, which had a 12-person marketing department to attract new business. Anthony's group regularly prepared pitches for clients.

"At first, I did a lot of mailings," Anthony said. "Preparing labels, things like that... There's a stigma about interns: 'Oh, he doesn't know anything; he's an intern.' In movies and on TV, people use 'intern' as a derogatory term."

Then one day Anthony's supervisor was out, and a very important RFP (Request For Proposal) came to his group. An extremely quick turnaround time complicated the situation. "One thing I've learned being at a law firm is that they wait till the very last second to tell you anything," Anthony said. "A lawyer approached our group around 1:00 and said that the RFP was needed by 2:30 for a meeting with a potential client.

"The big, big boss came by," Anthony said. "But it seemed like no one really believed that I could do it. They asked, 'Can you do it?' but they were quick to say 'If you think you can't handle it, we can always say that it's just not feasible for us to come up with the proposal today.'

"It was as if they didn't want to hurt my feelings," Anthony said. "But I knew I could do it. My boss had never given me the wheel on these projects, but I did have the opportunity to be a passenger." And he had paid close attention from the passenger's seat.

He proceeded to push out a quality proposal by 2:30. "I definitely felt the pressure, but I like pressure. And more than anything in the world, I love to prove people wrong when they think I can't do something."

The proposal helped the firm win that piece of business. "I got a lot more responsibility after that," Anthony said. "They realized I'm not an idiot. They got me involved in other RFPs. Now I'm in charge of maintaining inventory of items that we use for promotional events."

Still at the job on a part-time basis, Anthony reflected on the experience. "You always have to take the good with the bad; you have to earn your stripes," he said. "You have to prove yourself. No one is going to give you respect; you have to earn it. And I thrive on respect.

"You can't just talk about how great you are; you have to show it."

It boiled down to biding his time and being ready to jump in that driver's seat when a lesser person would have lacked the nerve to take the wheel.

Unpaid Evenings

About a month into his third and final co-op, Greg Fischer began talking to many of the large number of student employees that, like him, were new to the company, a large employer of engineering and business students. They all seemed to be on the same page. Given that they all had been there for a month, they didn't feel as ramped up as they should have been by that point. No one seemed to feel that they knew how to navigate such a large organization. And when someone did figure out how to accomplish something, how could everyone benefit from that so each individual wouldn't have to keep reinventing the wheel?

With the okay of his manager, Greg set out to create an "e-room," an electronic information repository for the many business units of the organization—a place where new co-ops could go to get immediate answers on any number of topics. There was general information about the organization—a Frequently Asked Questions (FAQ), a section on company policies, and more about locations. Then there were sections broken down by business unit, including background on that unit's mission, useful job-specific information, and even examples of completed work.

Around this time, Greg was asked if he would be willing to participate in information sessions that the company was holding on campus in a recruiting effort for the next co-op cycle. This was unpaid work for those who would attend, and they were held in the early evenings after a long day of work. "I wasn't even that interested in doing it," Greg told me. But he still did, and his career seemed to go into high gear as a direct result. One key individual gave him an opportunity to expand on his skills after those sessions, and Greg seized it. "You're really an employee here, not just a co-op or intern."

Now Greg is aggressively doing all he can to maximize the impact that his employer has on campus. He picked my brain about what other companies were doing and what lessons could be learned from those "best practices."

He's learned plenty of lessons without any help from me. "You need to be as proactive as you can be in asking questions," he says. "You may have communication skills, but you need to learn to use them."

"Talk to people," he added. "Speak up: Otherwise no one knows how smart or interested you are."

Greg seems poised for a great full-time position upon graduation. "It's awesome," he says. "I have the CIO and other senior managers telling me to be sure to interview for full-time jobs and to make sure I have meetings with them before going back to classes."

And those information sessions that Greg attended despite feeling only marginally enthusiastic about them? He now is entrusted to run these key events.

A Job Offer Without An Interview

How can you get a job offer without even interviewing for a job? Unless you're being handed a job by a friend or family member, that almost never happens. Case Western Reserve co-op coordinator Mary Rose Tichar passed along this story about a co-op who took an idea and really ran with it. This story is a good reminder of what a difference it can make to go the extra mile in your preparation. It also underscores the fact that many first-time professionals underrate the value of their transferable skills when pursuing their jobs in their fields.

I met electrical engineering student "Elias Inge" in his junior year as he prepared for his first co-op. During the first Prep Meeting for new co-ops, I briefly mentioned that creating a portfolio can be a good way to provide an illustration of your skills and what you have done. For students who may feel uncomfortable talking about themselves and their accomplishments, this can be a great way to communicate with an employer. I also wanted students to realize that their classroom projects and extracurricular activities can demonstrate soft skills such as creativity, teamwork, and organizational skills.

At the time, the portfolio was a new concept, especially for co-op students who didn't have much to put in a portfolio just yet. Well, Elias created one based on a research project he had done with a robot that demonstrated simple object avoidance behavior. He described the technology used for programming the robot. His portfolio included a colorful cover page, his resume, a project description with color photos for each aspect of the project. I was surprised and impressed.

Elias's friend was invited to a local company for an interview, and Elias asked him to take his portfolio and give it to the recruiter along with his resume. The recruiter was so impressed that he told the friend that Elias had a job too—with no interview! Elias had a great co-op at that company and impressed many with his creative and analytical approach to problem solving—qualities he had already displayed when submitting his portfolio to the hiring manager.

The Extra Mile

Years ago, Mary Jane Grusemeyer was a young graduate student who was helping out in business co-op. When a position became available to be a full-time marketing co-op coordinator, she decided to apply for it.

She came to me to work on her preparation, and she had her work cut out for her. Although she had amazing soft skills and a good relationship with a couple of people on the hiring committee, she had precious little corporate experience and not much experience in higher education either. I told her that for this position she likely would be one of the weakest candidates on paper. We set an ambitious but attainable goal for her interview: If she could come out of the group interview knowing that she had done everything in her power to deserve that position, then she could live with any outcome.

Still, she proceeded to go after the job as hard as humanly possible. She interviewed current and former marketing students. She tracked down the academic faculty and asked for their input on the co-op program. Mary Jane even arranged a meeting with some marketing co-op employers. Armed with all this information, she crafted a great interviewing strategy and went in and executed it. She stopped by afterwards on a real high. She had achieved her goal of doing everything she could do to get the job.

But she didn't get the job. Another candidate also interviewed very well, and that individual had many years of corporate sales experience and some background with higher education as well.

However, a couple of months later, a position became available in another co-op group. Members on that first committee went out of their way to let her know that it was available and to encourage her to apply. Mary Jane approached the interview just as she had before. This time around, all of the candidates were at a similar level of experience, and she absolutely blew away the competition. She went on to have a great career at Northeastern, then (as Mary Jane Miller) she went on to work at Purdue, and then Yale. But her first big break came when she trounced the competition by preparing more than anyone else would have thought possible.

Special Recognition
Northeastern nursing co-op coordinator Mary Carney told me about a first-time student of hers who I'll call "Natalie" here. Natalie accepted a job for her first co-op that Mary characterizes as "mundane." In other words, her duties were very simple—but essential—tasks. Unlike, say, a computer science student, many aspiring health care professionals cannot leap into the deep end of their profession when they first work as a co-op or intern. They aren't qualified to handle significant medical duties early on in their career.

Natalie's hospital job consisted of many low-skill tasks. She took blood pressure readings, bathed patients and assisted them with dressing, helped them get in and out of the bathroom, fetched slippers, made beds, and so forth. It was a job that an outsider easily could dismiss as one with a pretty minimal learning opportunity.

It didn't work out that way for Natalie. In the course of her humble duties, she befriended a patient in her mid-sixties, a woman who was scheduled for an aortic valve replacement. Any such procedure is not taken lightly, but it is not generally life-threatening either.

For various reasons—infections and the like—the surgery was delayed a few times. Natalie found that she really clicked with this woman and genuinely enjoyed a friendship with her. The night before her surgery, Natalie visited her to wish her well. Her new favorite patient talked happily about a wedding and vacation that she would enjoy after her surgery.

Things went very badly during surgery. The woman ended up in the intensive-care unit. Natalie visited her during breaks and after hours. She spent time with the family and comforted them as best she could.

The prognosis became very poor, but the situation continued for four or five days. The patient's daughter needed to go home. Natalie said she would stay. She slept on the couch in the family waiting room on the family's behalf.

Finally the patient's condition deteriorated, and she died. Natalie helped the family through the funeral arrangements, assisting with decisions such as whether to have an open or closed coffin. She attended the funeral—doing all of this on her own time. All of this happened nine months ago, and she remains in touch with the family.

Some time after things got back to normal at work for Natalie, there was a buzz in the air in her unit. Some of the most powerful people at the hospital had stopped by to personally express their appreciation for Natalie's above-and-beyond efforts. Even as an unlicensed member of the nursing staff—at one of the lowest levels of her organization—she was singled out for special recognition.

When she got back on campus, Natalie shared her experience with her fellow students, the academic faculty, and the co-op faculty. While everyone was impressed with her story, some cautioned her that she might need to be careful of burning out: A nurse can't afford to get this close to every patient. And some wondered if she had overstepped her boundaries. But the final verdict was that she needed to decide for herself as to how she felt about those issues.

Natalie heard everyone out but decided she would not have changed a thing. The experience profoundly influenced her professional development. She had begun her job as a mere provider of services. Now she knew what it meant to be a true health care professional.

CHAPTER FOUR

Do The Right Thing

Coming out of college, my father wanted to land a job in New York, New Jersey, or Connecticut. But besides some technical experience in the Navy, he had nothing much more going for him other than his new degree in electrical engineering. He needed serious job experience, and the best job he could land was a position in Indianapolis.

He never did like living there, but he had chosen wisely in terms of building a resume. A year or two later, he was able to beat out scores of candidates for a great engineering role in Connecticut. Eventually promoted to Chief Engineer, he appeared to be positioned for a good long-term career. The company had a profit-sharing plan, and my dad was impressed with how much that motivated people to manage costs carefully while doing quality work.

Then things changed. New management took over the company. To put it mildly, their policies contrasted sharply to those of the old regime. The profit-sharing plan was eliminated. As Chief Engineer, my father also started getting pressured to make decisions that made him uncomfortable. With new management looking to cut costs, my father was asked to lay off people against his will—individuals who he had hired and mentored. He also was asked to make compromises in terms of quality—shipping new products before they were ready just to meet an arbitrary deadline set by the new management.

When he expressed his discomfort with the situation, my father was given a few options. He could accept a demotion from Chief Engineer with an accompanying cut in pay—ending up working for someone who would enforce the new status quo. Or he could accept severance pay and leave the position.

My father had toyed with the idea of working on his own. He had a few ideas that he thought could work. Another plus was that it would spare one of his subordinates from being laid off. The right thing was to walk away from the job and run a business the way he felt it should be run.

Despite being disillusioned with his superiors, he took great care to leave the company on the best terms possible. As a direct result of that, he was able to do some freelance work for his company to bring in some money while getting his new company started. He also had earned the respect of many co-workers because of the way in which he handled the situation and treated everyone, and that also had a long-term payoff when many former co-workers came to work for him over the years.

Although optimistic about his career outlook, his entrepreneurial beginnings were humble. He was able to get some industrial loft space from a friend who ran another engineering firm. He didn't pay himself a dime for more than a year after beginning, living on that severance plus savings. Curiously, he and my mother described it as a real high point in their marriage—working together to get by on very little to get the fledgling business off the ground.

He hired one other employee and invented a safety device for industrial equipment. That did well, and he gradually built the business to the point where he could have a building constructed and then expanded for the growing corporation.

Many entrepreneurs would find his business philosophy counterintuitive. Repeatedly he resisted opportunities to grow the business quickly by borrowing money from banks, fearing that he could lose control of the business if things didn't go well. He believed that working much more than 40 hours per week would be a mistake: To be a productive engineer, he needed to have more balance in his life. So unlike most entrepreneurs, he would leave by 6 and enjoy tennis, gardening, woodworking, or home improvement projects.

He faced many times in which it was difficult to do the right thing. He agonized about having to let people go when the economy slowed down. He hated to put anyone out of work, and yet he realized that he couldn't do anyone any good if the business went under. During one particularly bad recession, he crunched the numbers and concluded that his payroll needed to be slashed by 20 percent in order to keep the business going. He finally came to a novel solution. Everyone at the company would cut their hours *and* their pay by 20 percent until things turned around. No one lost their job, and no one was forced to work the same number of hours for less pay—although many chose to do so.

Ultimately things turned around, and the company experienced many banner years throughout the 1980s—especially due to a control my dad designed for a large manufacturer of ice cream machines. Over the course of his career, he exemplified on several occasions how it was possible to do the right thing... and still do well. It's hard to imagine how his life would have turned out if he hadn't had the courage of his convictions back when his superiors put his job on the line and tried to force him to do things that he knew to be wrong.

The Fourth Key – Do The Right Thing

The fourth key to professional success is to do the right thing. Legendary civil rights pioneer Martin Luther King said:

"The ultimate measure of a man is not where he stands in moments of comfort and convenience, but where he stands at times of challenge and controversy."

Author Dante Alighieri reflected on this as well:

"The hottest places in Hell are reserved for those who in time of great moral crises maintain their neutrality."

Thomas Paine, one of the founding fathers of the United States, wrote:

"The harder the conflict, the more glorious the triumph. What we obtain too cheap, we esteem too lightly; it is dearness only that gives everything its value. I love the man that can smile in trouble, that can gather strength from distress and grow brave by reflection."

Eventually you're going to come to a crossroads in your career. You might become aware of something unethical—or even illegal—that a colleague or supervisor is doing at work. Even worse, you may know about it because *you* are being treated in an unethical or illegal way. Or you may just need to handle a significant difficulty that arises in your job—a disagreement with someone, a "problem personality" in the office, a boss with unreasonable expectations, a co-worker who unfairly takes credit for your accomplishments or blames you for things that may not be your fault. How do you deal with situations like these?

Elements of Doing The Right Thing

In digging through stories featuring themes related to doing the right thing, I identified the following components of this key to professional success:

1. Take the high road.
I often deal with students who have bottled up frustration or anger over how a co-worker, supervisor, or organization has treated them. It's not uncommon for people to fantasize about telling someone off at work or basically acting on their underlying aggressions in one way or another.

When talking to people pondering what to do about a conflict, my first advice is the following: "Whatever you do, you want to be able to look back on the situation and be able to feel proud of your actions." That means you need to be a class act—even when you're dealing with people who are anything but that. Don't do anything if you aren't confident that you'll be proud about how you opted to deal with it down the road.

2. Remember that the truth usually surfaces eventually.
Sometimes it's tough to see people get ahead at your organization by backstabbing, pandering to powerful people, bullying others, and so forth. Likewise, some people may be tempted to falsify their timesheets, tell "white lies" to extricate themselves from situations or to cast doubt over the performances of others.

Sometimes you are in a position where you might be able to do something about such unethical behaviors. In other situations, you might decide it's too risky to speak up. But don't succumb to the temptation of engaging in similar behavior. Remember that the truth often comes out sooner or later. That employee who is short-changing the organization is often discovered eventually, and people who have a habit of lying end up getting caught in their lies. When that happens, they lose credibility, fast.

3. Don't act impulsively.
When you're upset about something at work, the worst thing you can do is to speak up when you're emotions are running high. If you blurt something out, you run the risk of making an unfair assumption. If your actions or comments are going to generate *heat* without shedding much *light* on potential solutions, it's best to wait and think it through first.

4. Consider what might be gained or lost before deciding whether it's worthwhile to put a conflict on the table.
This directly follows from the previous point about acting impulsively. There are times when the best course of action is to confront a problem directly, but there may be times when bringing up an issue may get people upset without much hope of changing a situation for the better. Some good questions to ask yourself before you make a co-worker or supervisor aware of a problem:

- Can I raise this concern in a positive, solution-oriented manner, assuming the best of all involved if at all possible?
- Is it realistic to believe that something possibly can be done to make the situation better?
- What do I risk by bringing up this issue? Will I alienate someone who matters? Is the potential benefit worth the risk?

In and of itself, conflict is not a good or a bad thing. Too much conflict in a job situation is obviously a problem.... But too little conflict can be just as bad. If no one speaks up, some problems can increase in severity, affecting morale. It's definitely an art, finding ways to put problems on the table. But it's one that everyone needs to learn eventually.

5. Look to the best role models in your professional environment.
This is trickier than it appears to be. In almost every organization, there are exceptional performers and mediocre ones. Sometimes there are even truly terrible employees. Yet figuring out which is

which is not necessarily obvious. There are many pleasant and personable individuals who are great fun to talk to but who may be incompetent as professionals. Yet there may be others who are not remotely people whom you would choose as friends in everyday life but who have a great deal to teach you as professionals.

It's best to assume that everyone you work with may have something of value to teach you. By talking to people about their roles, you often can take away *something* that you might want to emulate. You also may learn what behaviors to avoid. Above all, though, you want to make sure that you don't assume that a given behavior is okay or good just because you see someone else engaging in that behavior in your workplace. You could end up emulating someone who actually is held in low regard or who even may be close to termination.

True Stories about Doing The Right Thing

The Conference-Call Explosion

When you work with an individual who is basically a cancer in your organization, it can be very tempting to tell that person off or sink down to their level. In the following story, Northeastern University alum Keith Laughman describes a situation in which he had every justifiable reason to be furious at a co-worker. Yet he still describes his resulting conference-call tirade as the most regrettable moment of his career.

Whether you are a co-op or intern, recent graduate, or 15-year veteran of your industry, there are going to be times when you want to blow up at a fellow employee. Take it from me: Control yourself. Why do I know this, you may ask? One time I gave in to that temptation, and I now view it as the blackest mark on my career.

You'll meet a ton of new and interesting people on your career journey. Some of them you will like; others are people you know you will not be friends with from the first day you meet them. Either way, you have to respect them and work with them.

So let me tell you about "Jim," my former co-worker. Jim was a heavy-set individual who loved to take cigarette breaks for an hour at a time—up to three times a day, not including lunch. He would stroll into work at about 7 a.m. to beat the morning traffic and—without fail—be out of the office by 2 p.m. His hours were a running joke. When we bought clocks to display the different time zones for which we had to provide technology support, I had one left over and dubbed it "EJT" (Eastern Jim Time). We set the time to be 1:45 p.m. and took the batteries out of it. That was his "clock-out time," and there was no accounting for daylight savings! When Jim wasn't on a break, he usually would be checking the top sports-related websites. It was no secret that Jim wasn't up on his technical knowledge and that he was kept around because he was buddies with some of the managers.

We were system engineers and responsible for supporting sophisticated computer hardware. The job was pretty stressful, especially when things were broken and users were screaming at you. Over the years, Jim had adopted many habits—not answering his cellphone when required, passing numerous problems onto others, and in general being completely unreliable. As time progressed, I could see why people would start to lose their patience with Jim. In fact, it may sound like I'm making this whole story up. Unfortunately, it's true.

One day our department took on one of the largest projects to come across our organization in several years. They were looking for a project manager to drive this giant conversion from one operating system platform to another. Apparently someone said, "Why not Jim?" He became the project lead for this 18-month long project. Most of us thought he would wake up and he would start applying himself. He did the opposite. He failed to communicate with his team, forgot about deadlines, fought with other administrators, and threw some of them under the bus to cover his own mistakes.

This is where I come in. Many of the admins had fights on a daily basis with Jim. Ninety-nine percent of the time I kept my mouth shut and didn't get involved, but once I did not do that. We were on a conference call on a Monday afternoon, and I had just worked about 45 hours nonstop over the weekend to ensure the successful migration of a sophisticated database. I got no sleep.

During the phone call, there were a couple arguments between our employees and the consultants. It came to light that a task had not been done: Jim had not delegated it to anyone. This wasn't his first miscommunication or costly mistake. Yet even on this fourth migration, Jim was *still* not getting the job done and our group was suffering because of it.

When this overlooked task was brought up, naturally everyone looked at me as if I were to blame. I pride myself on being prepared and thorough in my execution of tasks. This was a huge task that ended up affecting the daily business of several hundred users, so it had high visibility. As a result, I immediately got defensive and stated that there had been no documentation of this task needing to be done and that no one had sent it to me.

Jim and I started to argue about it in front of everyone. I had my laptop with me, and I showed Jim I was never sent an e-mail on it. As if to brush that off, Jim proceeded to say that I *should have* known to do it if I was at all knowledgeable about the migration or my job. Can you believe it? This from a man who spent most of his days on cigarette breaks or surfing the net! That was the straw that broke my back—the way he had humiliated me because he couldn't accept his own responsibility. And he did so in front of vendors, on a conference call with our global counterparts, and in front of my peers (who knew the real story).

This is where I wish I had chosen to be the bigger man. Instead, I proceeded to stop the debate on the conference call and proclaim my innocence while raising my voice and getting in some choice words with Jim. The whole floor could hear me. I was swearing and shouting, and then I got personal and attacked his character and knowledge. This went on for about ten minutes. People were shocked, and the call ended shortly after we walked away from the meeting in opposite directions.

What was I to do? You might think that I had every right to explode after dealing with this over a long period of time. WRONG! There are other ways that this situation could have been handled before it reached that ugly point. The correct answer is not to rip into the person in a public debacle of profanity, but rather to seek an alternate method. Have a closed-door session with your manager and a problem employee, or approach Human Resources if it's that upsetting.

Eventually you will come across a co-worker who will upset you and make work much more difficult for you. With these people, you need to practice a higher degree of self-control and make sure that you do not lose your temper. Document the problems, keep your cool, and approach it from a different angle.

If I could go back and change one career decision in my life, it would be this one. From that point on, work wasn't the same. Neither was I. I had done things that I never wanted to do in my professional life. Keep this story in the back of your mind and remember it the next time you want to go off on one of your co-workers. Since that experience, I have always looked for an alternate route in dealing with issues, and they all have been resolved much more smoothly.

This was an ugly day for me and my career. Don't make the same mistake I did.

Rat Trap?

I didn't hear about this conflict until well after the student resolved it without any assistance from me whatsoever. "Harry Nowitzky" had a nice job working in software and hardware support for one of our prominent co-op employers. Everything was going great until a problem with a co-worker emerged one day. Then Harry agonized about how to handle a real dilemma.

Harry had been asked to do the "back end" work needed to update virus protection for dozens of computers in the HR and Marketing Departments at the office. A full-time worker was supposed to finish the task by making sure that he took the software Harry had added to the network and ensured that it actually got onto each employee's desktop and worked correctly.

A day or two after completing his end of the project, Harry called the co-worker to verify that the second phase had been completed. "Actually, no," the guy said, to Harry's surprise. "I had some problems getting it to work, so I finally just got frustrated and bagged it."

After hanging up the phone, Harry felt an incredible degree of anxiety about what to do next. He didn't want to run to his boss and "rat" on his full-time colleague, as he worried how it would affect his relationship with this person. However, if he didn't do anything, and a virus crashed the network, then there might be hell to pay for both of them. Or would it only reflect on the other guy? He wondered if he should let the situation play out.

Finally he decided what to do. He would "assume the best" of his co-worker and make his boss aware of the situation while giving his co-worker the benefit of the doubt as much as he could. He told his boss that the co-worker had not completed the task but added "You know, he very well could be intending to get back to that and make sure it happens—maybe he was just frustrated when I talked to him. He might have a solution in mind by now."

His manager thanked him. "If someone in that group downloads something they shouldn't—and you just know they will sooner or later—then we're all in trouble over here, including me!" Harry came away knowing he'd done the right thing while being as fair as possible to his fellow employee.

E is for Evidence

At a recent training on campus to build awareness about sexual harassment, the facilitator who ran the session asked us if anyone knew what the "e" in "e-mail" *really* stands for. A few people had good guesses, such as "everlasting" or "eternal"—meaning that once you write something and send it via e-mail, you'd better assume that it's going to be around forever.

But the facilitator also reminded us that "e" also stands for "evidence." What you write in any e-mail could be used as evidence against you legally or in terms of your employment record.

A good example of this comes to mind. A few years back, "Theresa Taileffer" was a student of mine who was winding down her job search. In fact, she had accepted a job offer. Shortly thereafter, another employer of mine e-mailed her to offer a position working for him. Theresa promptly wrote back with a polite and professional e-mail, letting him know that she'd accepted another position.

Here's how he responded to that e-mail: "Wow, congratulations on getting that job! I'm sure that will work out great for you... Actually, maybe it's just as well that you accepted that job. To be honest, I found you very, very attractive during the interview process, and it might have affected my ability to make a fair judgment about who to hire! I guess what I'm trying to say is that I was wondering if you'd like to have dinner with me some time?"

Theresa wasn't too upset about it... but she simply hit the

"Forward" button so I would see the e-mail. As a note, she added, "I'm not going to respond to this. I figured I'd just forward it to you, and you'd know how to handle it."

So what did I do? I didn't think that the guy was harassing Theresa; I thought that he was just trying to flatter her in a clumsy—and stupid—way. What could have possessed him to imply that his professional judgment was compromised when a pretty face appeared in front of him? After mulling it over, I forwarded the e-mail to my HR contact at his company to make sure someone would talk to him about it with the goal of avoiding a similar mistake in the future. I'm sure that led to a very embarrassing conversation—all because he didn't think of e-mail as "everlasting" or as "evidence."

Truth and Consequences

One major challenge in my job is that a co-op coordinator has to be the liaison between students and employers. When there is a conflict between the two, each party usually expects me to side with them. With two different perspectives, it can be quite difficult to figure out the truth when something goes very wrong.

"Boris Chernov" was on his second six-month co-op with one of my key employers. One day someone from Human Resources called me up to inform me that Boris had been fired. They claimed that he had falsified his timesheets for several weeks, defrauding the company out of several thousand dollars. The HR contact was furious and demanded that I do everything I could to get him expelled from Northeastern immediately. I told her I would need to hear his side of the story before I could do anything. She was not pleased with me.

Sure enough, Boris denied everything. He claimed that there was someone in the mailroom who disliked him because he was Russian-born; he said that this mailroom employee told him that he should go back to his own country. He suspected that this employee had monkeyed with his timesheets to get him in trouble. Now Boris wanted me to send his resume to another employer as soon as possible. I told him that we couldn't do that until I fully understood what had happened with his employer. Now Boris was not happy with me either!

Gradually, the truth came out. If Boris was saying that someone falsified his timesheets, then he was agreeing that he had received much bigger checks than he was supposed to receive. Hadn't he noticed that?

"I have direct deposit on my paychecks," he said. "I didn't check the amounts after I made sure they were getting deposited the first time. And that money goes into a separate account that I only use for paying tuition, so I haven't noticed."

I was becoming skeptical but went along with it. Then I had a brainstorm. "This is great!" I said. "I know a great way to clear your name: Tomorrow, bring me a certified bank check for the full amount that you were overpaid. And bring me your bank statement so we can see that there was no other activity in the account for the last three months!"

Boris agreed to do so, but his lack of enthusiasm and pale face said it all. He didn't have that amount of money—not anymore—nor could he produce the bank records.

In the end, he was suspended and not allowed to return to classes until he had repaid the full amount to the employer. As you would expect, I was through with him. Worst of all, though, that employer had provided him with ALL of the corporate experience that he had gained thus far in his career. What could he do? His choices were to put the employer on his resume and face the anxiety of what a typical reference check would reveal... or he could leave it off his resume and have no significant experience. And he would have to explain why there was such a big gap of time on his resume.

This kind of situation is rare, but it does happen. If your own code of ethics or morals doesn't keep you from doing something like this, I would hope that the gravity of the consequences would make you hesitate. In the big picture, Boris gambled—and lost—a great deal for the sake of a few thousand dollars.

A "Friend" In Need

My student "Oliver Englert" learned several tough lessons during the first year I worked with him. For starters, he went on about 11 interviews before getting an offer, working hard to contain his frustration after being named the "runner-up" or "alternative choice" for several positions but never getting them.

That part of the story seemed to end happily. Interview #12 led to a job, and Oliver was quick to tell me that it actually was the best of all the jobs he had pursued. So I thought he was all set. But that's just where this story begins.

Oliver worked for a financial services organization downtown. It was his first experience in the professional world, and he was eager to achieve and belong. He had an excellent relationship with his supervisor, and he ended up learning a great deal.

But several months into the job, something unexpected happened. His manager called him into his office. "I want to ask you for a favor, Oliver," his boss said. Oliver figured it might be coming in on a weekend again—he had done that before. Instead, the manager asked him if he could borrow $1,000 from him. His boss was trying to buy a house and needed to put together enough for the down payment.

Oliver was surprised but quickly agreed to help out his manager. They were friends, after all. But within a matter of weeks, the company became aware that Oliver's supervisor was asking a number of direct reports for large loans. He was terminated on the spot.

Oliver looked kind of shell-shocked as he told me all of this. I told him that what he did may have been unwise but that he certainly was not the guilty party here. He had done nothing wrong; it was his manager who had abused power and taken advantage of him quite unfairly. Oliver nodded but seemed unconvinced. "HR told me the same thing," he said. "It's just that I feel so ashamed of myself. How could I have been so naïve?"

Although he ultimately got his money back, that didn't make Oliver feel much better. What hurt so much was feeling like a *real* professional would have known better. That's why I tell you this story. If someone in a professional setting asks something of you that makes you feel uncomfortable or makes you wonder if you're engaging in unwise, unethical, or illegal behavior, it's important to get someone else's opinion on the matter. Ask your co-op or career services professional if you obtained your job through your school. If not, talk to someone you can trust in HR or in a position of authority at your organization. You don't want to find out the hard way that someone else took unfair advantage of you in the workplace.

A Hands-On Manager

Fortunately, I have only had to deal with sexual harassment issues a handful of times over a decade-plus of working with young employees and employers. Probably the worst one I ever had was about six years ago, when I received an e-mail marked "URGENT... CONFIDENTIAL" from "Susanna Hagi," who had been in a job for about four months.

She had gone to lunch a couple of times with her boss's boss—just trying to develop a network of contacts. But things had evolved, and now she was very uncomfortable. She told me that this guy made several female employees uneasy because of his tendency to hug people affectionately quite often. She attributed that to his cultural background and tried not to think about it. But then he started talking about wanting to get involved with her. She told him she wasn't interested. When he persisted, she even took a picture of her husband out of her wallet and said, "Look, I'm *married*." The guy said, "So what? So am I."

When he drove her back to the office and wouldn't drop the topic, she threatened to tell someone. He slammed on the brakes. "You will *not* tell anyone about this!" he said. She became afraid that she would lose her job if she spoke up. So even though I visited her a few weeks later and asked how things were going, she said that everything was fine.

Eventually a co-worker—another student of mine—convinced her to talk to me about it. In our first conversations, Susanna blamed herself. "I never should've gone to lunch with him," she said. A female colleague of mine and I talked to her at length and gradually convinced her that she had not "asked for trouble" by going to lunch. It took a while, but Susanna finally got angry about it, realizing how unfair and controlling this manager had been. But she was still reluctant to do anything about it besides talking to my colleague and me—she was afraid of losing her otherwise good job.

Finally she decided that this man had to be stopped—otherwise he would keep doing this kind of thing to others. She had heard that she had not been the only one he had propositioned. So she went to Human Resources and told her story. When the manager heard about the complaint, he denied everything, naturally. But the conclusion was that the HR manager told the guy the following: "Okay, fine... We'll give you the benefit of the doubt because it's your word against hers. But if it happens again, it will be a different story."

Certainly Susanna didn't want to have to experience something like this. But she did walk away from the job with a feeling of pride: Although it was hard, she very well may have saved other young women from unwanted advances.

To Tell The Truth

It's embarrassing to me to share some of the "horror stories" that I've dealt with in my many years of working with college students, but I do so in the hope that others will learn from some of their mistakes.

Many years ago I had a student that I will call "Lauren Ecclestone" for our purposes here. Lauren had her first interview at one of my top employers ever, and I was pretty stunned at the phone call I received from the company afterwards. My HR contact told me that Lauren had been "making out" with her boyfriend in the waiting area prior to the interview!

As you might imagine, I called Lauren and asked her about it. She admitted that her boyfriend had accompanied her to the interview "to hold my hand because I was nervous" but adamantly denied that they had even kissed. Stuck in the middle, I called my contact back and asked who had seen this. As luck would have it, the witness to this display was a former student of mine and a co-op award winner to boot. In fact, it was someone that I've written about elsewhere in this book!

I called him up and told him that Lauren had said that he must have been mistaken in what he saw. "No way," he said. "I walked into the waiting area, and they were going at it on the couch. They jumped about a foot when they noticed me and quickly separated."

I met with Lauren and told her what my alum had said. She still denied it. I decided to let it go with the exception of telling her that it was absolutely inappropriate for her to bring a boyfriend, friend, family member, or ANYONE with her to an interview. She agreed to this and got a job—somewhere else.

The next time around things appeared to be going smoothly. She got a really good job in downtown Boston and started in late June. Within a few weeks, though, she met with me. She told me she needed to quit because her grandmother in South America was terribly ill and that she and her mother needed to go down there to take care of her through the rest of the summer. It seemed odd to me that it would be necessary for both of them to go, but I accepted the explanation. So she quit the job, and I had to deal with an unhappy employer.

A year later, though, another student ended up in that same job that Lauren had quit. By coincidence, she eventually met Lauren in a class and got talking, and the two of them realized that they had had the same job. "Oh yeah," Lauren told her. "I decided I didn't want that job after all, so I quit really soon after I started." The other student was appalled and told me about it. The end result: It was obvious to me that Lauren had lied to me twice, and she permanently lost me as a personal reference on top of alienating two of the biggest employers in her field in the Boston area.

More often than people realize, the truth comes out eventually in a long-term relationship. Lauren's poor judgment in each case was a problem that she compounded by lying about what had happened. At the moment, it probably seemed convenient to avoid the truth, but she burned bridges with many people because of her actions. You can recover from most mistakes in your career, but once you lose trust, it is hard to regain it.

Two Angry Men

One morning years ago, I picked up our student newspaper and couldn't believe something that I read. An article talked about students who goofed off at work, and one of my students was quoted in it! "I got away with so much," Management Information

Systems major "Kevin Maloney" boasted. "I spent most of time surfing the net to check out espn.com."

I was angry and embarrassed. He was actually bragging about not doing work... and he had fully identified himself, right down to his major. So the next time he came in, I let him know how it had angered me to see that in print.

"Well, I'm angry, too," he said. "That job was a joke! But I should explain about the newspaper article. They misquoted me; they made it sound like I was proud of the fact that I wasn't doing anything. It wasn't as if I was happy to have so little to do."

"Okay," I said. "But if you had nothing to do, why didn't you call me or e-mail me? I would've rather found out you were unhappy that way instead of reading it in the newspaper... And speaking of which, you're telling me you're *surprised* that you were misquoted in a student newspaper? It's not as if you were talking to *The New York Times* or *The Boston Globe...*"

Now *he* looked embarrassed. "Yeah, I realize that now," he said glumly. "And I should've called you, I guess. I just figured that there was nothing that you could do about it."

"Maybe that would've been the case," I said. "But I would have liked the opportunity to try."

Kevin apologized, and I told him I was sorry that he was disappointed in the job—although I also added that I thought the job would benefit him when it came time for his next job search. Then I wrapped up our meeting the way I try to conclude any meeting in which strong words have been exchanged. "Okay, I think we've learned all that we can learn about what happened," I said. "We've dealt with it directly and both said things that needed to be said. So now we're going to move forward and leave this behind us. I'm not going to keep reminding you about this situation for the whole rest of the time you're at Northeastern. I appreciate that you were willing to talk this through me."

I worked with Kevin for the next two years—very successful ones for him. Sure enough, the issue never arose again, and we had a great relationship based on mutual respect. He had been willing to communicate directly about a bad situation and to take responsibility for some bad decisions on his part, and this helped us clear the air and move on pretty quickly.

I have one footnote to this story. In a very unlikely coincidence, I bumped into Kevin at a wedding reception for two other NU alums just a few days before this book went to print. He talked with great fondness about his co-op career and with true pride in Northeastern University.

Reflecting on this story, I couldn't resist asking him how he now felt about that first job he had. I was pleased to hear that he now looks at it as a "terrific first experience"—not so much from a technical skill-building standpoint but more from the sense of learning the fundamentals of being an employee in a workplace every day. He also emphasized that there was no way he would have been able to obtain his excellent *second* job without that first job, which turned out to be the starting point for a career that continues to be very satisfying.

A Costly Meal

There are some stories in this book that reflect so badly on those involved that I'm not going to identify what university the students attended, let alone any other remotely recognizable details.

Several years ago I heard about a pretty amazing example of selfishness. There was a nationally-renowned employer who had terrific co-ops... but they were in an unusual location. To attract great students, the employer provided free housing, free rental cars, multiple round-trip airfares, and many other amazing perks for co-ops and interns.

Unfortunately, there were so many perks that it seemed to create a sense of entitlement with some of the co-ops. I heard of some students complaining because their rental car was not quite as new as everyone else's. I heard of one student who got fired for poor performance and then was amazed to learn that he couldn't just stay in the free housing for the rest of the "work" term!

But the very worst of all involved three students who were wrapping up their time with the employer. Human Resources told them that they would need to move out of their free housing a day before their scheduled flight. To make up for this inconvenience, HR booked rooms for the students at a hotel near the airport. "There's a good restaurant right in the hotel," the HR rep told the trio. "You can have dinner there, and the company will pick up the tab."

You can guess what happened. Whenever I ask students to guess how big the tab was, they always guess too low. If I recall correctly, the bill was something like $700 for the dinner—and that was in the late 1990s. I still wonder whether there was an Endangered Species Mixed Grill or something like that on the menu. More likely, it was a case of three young people who had become a little too used to the perks. They figured that they were leaving anyway; why not run up a huge tab by ordering the most expensive entrees and a few premium bottles of wine as well? What difference would it make?

It made a big difference as it turned out. Word got around, and their references from the employer were history. So was that company's hiring program with that school. And you can imagine what it did to their relationships with the people back at their university who helped them get the job.

Quitting Time

I talked to one of my young alums recently. About a year ago, he left the first full-time job that he received upon graduation. In the process, he learned many valuable lessons in ethics, diplomacy, and priorities.

I will call him "Steve Prentiss." Steve was a superstar co-op employee, and he received a high-paying full-time job from his big-name employer after completing his last co-op with that company. For the next two years, he put in long hours on some major projects, and the understanding was that he would be compensated generously for the extra effort eventually... and also that he would be able to move into a different role if he so desired in the future.

Finally, the project was completed, but the euphoria in his group quickly gave way to disappointment. The promised bonuses did not come through, and the group was demoralized. Steve decided that maybe it was time to seek a different role within the company, but he was told that he would need to stay in his group for the foreseeable future. "We don't have a place elsewhere in the company for you right now," a manager said to him.

Steve tried to accept that, but other signs disturbed him. Various perks and extras were slashed from the budget; office doors that always been open were suddenly shut. Steve started thinking of one corridor as "Depression Row." Now that his efforts to turn things around for himself within the company had been rebuffed, he started thinking about an external search. Given that he had been there full-time for two years—most professionals will tell you that it's rarely a good idea to leave a job unless you've been there for a minimum of a full year—he felt he should explore external options.

But this posed ethical and practical problems for him as well. He feared that if he made his desire to leave the company known to all, he might suffer for it: It could affect his job responsibilities, his raises, and his performance evaluations. So he kept it quiet. Fortunately, he had a good network of contacts from his previous co-op jobs; he could now use them as references. Ethically, he also knew it would be wrong to short-change his employer by conducting a job search on company time. So he conducted phone interviews at lunch, worked on resumes and cover letters in the evenings, and used vacation days or personal days to go on interviews.

Before long he landed another job and had to tell his current manager that he would be leaving. It was a very nerve-wracking experience. His manager was shocked. Steve wisely gave his employer more than two weeks' notice and even offered to train someone on his responsibilities. Then he followed up with an e-mail so there would be a written record of the meeting and the agreed-upon last day.

So far, so good, but then his manager's manager took it very poorly and got very angry at Steve for leaving. That person yelled at Steve, and it wasn't a good time to try to have a productive conversation about what had happened and why. So Steve waited... and then approached that individual a week later to clear the air. Steve explained all of his reasons for leaving and how he had first tried to make it work with an internal move. By the end of the conversation, Steve believed that what he had accomplished was "huge." He felt able to walk away from the job with a minimum of hurt feelings.

Some conversations are never easy to have, and some conflicts are easy to bury rather than putting them on the table. You can't always control how someone might react when you say things that they may not want to hear. That said, you still want to do everything in your power to be able to walk away from a job or a conflict knowing in your heart that you did the right thing and were as fair as possible to all parties while being true to yourself.

CHAPTER FIVE

See The Big Picture

My job years ago as a medical writer and project manager seemed to go great until I got promoted. During my first year, I probably had been given more credit than I deserved for many successful projects. I had a reasonable workload, and my boss always seemed to assume the best of me. That made it easy to go to work motivated. I also liked the challenge. I had been asked to become the company's immunology expert, and I did well at mastering that relatively abstract element of medicine.

I should have known that the party would be over once I was promoted. I had seen it happen to several peers. Once in more of a management role, these colleagues faced much heavier workloads. When projects went well, much of the credit seemed to go to the writers who produced the end product. When something went wrong, it seemed that it was the project manager's fault. I even had been promoted to replace someone who once had been held in high esteem but then ended up getting criticized left and right. Somehow I thought it would be different for me.

It wasn't. We were short-staffed when it came to managers,

and we reached a point where I was doing just about all of the project-related travel for the company. Yet I was supposed to be managing major projects back in the office as well—including a million-dollar project for which I was given no internal staff writers. I had to hire a whole team of freelancers and try to get their writing to hold together, even though none of them worked in our offices at all.

I started burning out. It was the kind of place where people would make a "joking" comment when you left before 7 p.m. "Working half a day today?" they would say as you headed for the door. Even working over 60 hours per week, I couldn't possibly do all that really needed to be done without sacrificing key steps that would ensure quality. I tried to convince the owner that we needed to hire another manager; the response was "We'll see..."

I noticed that my attitude changing. At one time I had enjoyed a great relationship with the editorial staff, but my treatment of co-workers became characterized by impatience. With so much hanging over me, it felt like a waste of time to really listen to people's concerns or to maintain rapport through small talk.

Within nine months of receiving the promotion, I was tempted to just quit in a huff. I could imagine how satisfying it would be to tell off the boss and make them scramble to get my work done. *Then* they would realize how much I handled and how impossible my job was!

Fortunately, I did nothing of the sort. I talked to my mentor Jan Wohlberg, my supervisor from my teaching days at Boston University and co-author of my first textbook. She reminded me that I had everything to gain by taking the high road and leaving on the best terms possible.

It was a matter of seeing the big picture. In the heat of the moment, it was difficult to think beyond extricating myself from a job that had been great but had become extremely unenjoyable. Some people thrive on working 60 or 70 hours per week, but I am not one of them. I'm not good at working on one thing for 12 hours a day and then going home, having dinner, watching TV, and going to bed. I need more balance in my life.

The more I reflected on the situation, I was able to see it for what it really was. If I could leave on great terms, I could come away with a great reference instead of burning bridges. And as I didn't have too much job experience at that point, I might need that reference.

Another realization was that although I had become unhappy in the job, my hard work resulted in many terrific projects that I could put on my resume as well as finished products that I could put in a portfolio. I could stay in touch with the people who had become my friends at the company while not having to deal with others who had not.

Still, I was nervous about telling the owner. We both knew that there were tensions between us. I told her that I had decided that it was time to move on. But I added that I could be very flexible about how that happened. "I don't want to leave anyone in the lurch, so I'd be happy to stick around a while to complete the projects that I'm managing. But if you want me to pack up my desk and finish today, I could do that too. Or I could work from home if that helps—I know you have space issues here."

The owner just seemed to relax completely. "How about this?" she said. "Why don't you make a list of the projects that you think would be best for you to complete?" she suggested. I readily agreed, and from then on all the tension between us just seemed to evaporate.

I don't think I even realized how much the job situation affected me till weeks later. I got my wife laughing one night, and she said,

"Hey! Your sense of humor came back!"

I was stunned. "You mean it went away?"

She thought about it a little longer and then nodded. I got back into consulting work after that and honed my writing skills on the side. Eventually I sought full-time work again and ended up with a job offer from a renowned publishing company as well as the one I took at Northeastern. My old boss indeed received a call for a reference and gave me a great one: She seemed genuinely enthusiastic and saw it as a great fit for me.

I don't look back too fondly on my last nine months in that job, but it was a powerful learning experience for me. I learned that if you no longer believe that you can be committed to doing your best in a job—and if you've been there a minimum of one year—then you need to move on as graciously as possible.

Now my experience in that job proves very valuable to me as I counsel students about tough work environments, fickle supervisors, and so forth.

When you're facing adversity in the workplace, it is all too easy to get immersed in the immediate challenges. But you have to remember that short-term sacrifices can pay off and that everything in your career is subject to change... in the big picture.

The Fifth Key – See The Big Picture

The fifth key to professional success is to see the big picture. Albert Einstein said:

"In the middle of every difficulty lies opportunity."

In his classic *Letters To A Young Poet*, early 20th-century poet Rainer Maria Rilke said:

"I would like to beg you dear Sir, as well as I can, to have patience with everything unresolved in your heart and to try to love the questions themselves as if they were locked rooms or books written in a very foreign language. Don't search for the answers, which could not be given to you now, because you would not be able to live them. And the point is to live everything. Live the questions now. Perhaps then, someday far in the future, you will gradually, without even noticing it, live your way into the answer."

Psychiatrist M. Scott Peck, author of *The Road Less Traveled,* said:

"The truth is that our finest moments are most likely to occur when we are feeling deeply uncomfortable, unhappy, or unfulfilled. For it is only in such moments, propelled by our discomfort, that we are likely to step out of our ruts and start searching for different ways or truer answers."

In the course of my work, I occasionally talk to students who received poor work evaluations or who have been terminated from their jobs. Some of these people are quick to tell me that they would have done a great job... if they only were given great things to do.

My response usually begins as follows: "In my experience, I would say that a mediocre employee can do a great job in a role that he or she loves. But a great employee gets a great evaluation for a job that he or she might not have liked."

While this is true, what is it, exactly, that separates the two kinds of individuals? In my opinion, it is the ability to see the big picture. On the one hand, there are people who tend to believe that their work is only meaningful if they are engaged in tasks that directly relate to their future career goals. Anything other than that has little or no value in the estimation of people with that outlook.

Conversely, there are those who have an uncanny knack of finding meaning and importance in whatever they do. These are people who realize that there's so much to learn at work that has *nothing to do with your field*. How do you learn the unwritten rules at work? How do you "manage" your manager? Learning time management, juggling multiple tasks, developing contacts through networking... There are countless ways in which just about any job aids your professional development. But if you're convinced that there's nothing to learn, then guess what? You'll learn nothing.

Seeing the big picture also means that you won't always receive immediate gratification of your goals and desires. Few people are handed great jobs on a platter: They have to earn their opportunities. The more attractive the goal, the longer it may take to reach it—and there may be major sacrifices to make if it's going to happen. Are you willing to do that? If not, you may need a new goal.

No one can predict the future. That's what makes seeing the big picture one of the most difficult steps. Who knows just how valuable your coursework or a given job experience will prove to be a decade or two from now? I never thought that the intensive biology course I took as a college freshman would pay off, but then I never imagined I would become a medical writer. When I began writing case studies while teaching at BU, I didn't know that this would lead directly to co-authoring my first textbook. When I started creating written materials on resume writing and interviewing at Northeastern, I sure didn't know that I would end up putting them in my *Find Your First Professional Job* textbook.

So perhaps the moral of this chapter is that you need to do your best and trust that hard work pays off, both handsomely and unexpectedly. You just have to be open to the idea that your experiences—good and bad—always bring growth, whether or not you realize it. The best professionals find a way to make sure that they milk every experience for all its worth.

Elements of Seeing The Big Picture

In assembling the stories featuring themes related to seeing the big picture, I came up with several elements that comprise this key to professional success:

1. Be open to change.
The best career path to take is not always the most convenient one. People tend to fear change, preferring the comfort of their current situation—even when they are not very happy. Sometimes you need to be willing to take a reasonable risk in life—moving somewhere new, taking on tasks without total certainty of whether you can be successful, or accepting that you've made a mistake or gone in the wrong direction.

Another piece of advice I often give: When in doubt about what to choose, pick something that will open doors for you in the future... even if you're not sure what rooms are beyond those doors! That's what Rilke meant when he referred to the need to "live your way into the answer." As much as you might like to have a five or ten-year plan, sometimes you just have to live life and see where it leads you.

2. What appears to be a step backward might be a prelude to two steps forward.
I can't begin to estimate how many times I have heard of someone who went into a professional environment and emerged disappointed because they learned that they were in the wrong field. People commonly perceive this development as a failure. Instead, it's a huge step closer to finding the right career by ruling out the wrong one.

Likewise, I have met innumerable people who ultimately realized that the worst or most difficult job they ever had eventually turned out to be one of the profound learning experiences of their careers. If you ever dealt with a terrible manager, miserable co-workers, or a hostile work environment, it has a permanent impact on what you value in a job or organization. It's not always obvious until the experience is distant in the rearview mirror, but wait for it! The learning potential is enormous—unless you dismiss that possibility.

3. Make short-term decisions that will benefit you in the long run.
Although it doesn't happen too often, I always roll my eyes when a student tells me that she or he wants a job that is in downtown Boston... close to public transportation... and preferably within walking distance of the university. Of course, it had better be a high-paying job as well.

"Well, I would hope that your primary goal is to get a job that will be a terrific learning experience and a great resume builder," I say, once I have stopped sighing and reestablished eye contact.
Don't get me wrong: I've got nothing against good pay and a convenient commute! It's just that when you're starting your career, it's best to have the attitude that you'll work wherever the best opportunity is. If you get a better job now, it will tee you up for better pay and more opportunities down the road.

4. Don't flee situations when you face the first hurdle.
Increasingly, I have to deal with students who run into a challenge or hurdle in the first weeks of a new job and whose immediate gut reaction is to want to quit. It boggles my mind. It's analogous to a baseball player who strikes out his first time up... and then just decides to quit the sport on the spot.

So why do we see more of this these days? Maybe we have provided a little too much support to some members of the Millennial Generation. Parents and teachers have always been there to solve the problems, and for some that has meant stopping any activity if it doesn't bring almost immediate gratification. Or perhaps some young professionals grew up engaging in many activities—soccer, swimming, karate, day camps—that required a commitment of only a handful of weeks. And if you weren't having fun within those few weeks, you just opted out after that point.

Quitting a job—or bailing out on any relationship—should almost never be a first resort with the exception of situations that involve abuse or harassment. And I can count on one hand the number of times I have had that happen in 11 years in cooperative education. There can be significant learning when you have to find a positive way to confront a problem and overcome it instead of running from it.

True Stories about Seeing The Big Picture

All Work and No Pay

Genevieve Jewell was one of my General Management students looking for a six-month job from July through December 2005. With a great GPA, good job experience, and terrific soft skills, Genevieve was qualified for many high-paying co-op jobs. But her heart was set on her own dreams, no matter how much I told her about how hard it would be to fulfill them. I would try to tempt her with other job descriptions, but she was resolute—despite knowing what sacrifices it would entail. Her story in her own words follows.

I was always told that making it in the entertainment industry would not be an easy thing to do. It is known in the co-op world as the "sexy industry" that everyone wants to get into. Well, I was determined to make myself a future in it and my second co-op ended up leading me to a career in the music industry.

I decided I wanted to get an internship in the music industry. I sent out many resumes and made numerous phone calls, encountering rejection again and again. After searching for companies on the Internet one day, I came across a large artist management company called Nettwerk Management. Their client roster includes Avril Lavigne, Barenaked Ladies, Sarah McLachlan, Dido, Hem, Guster, and many other artists. So I decided to call Nettwerk to find out to whom I should address a cover letter.

After being told that they do not take intern resumes, I decided to take matters into my own hands. I was able to find out the name of Sarah McLachlan's personal manager, and I decided to send my resume straight to her. I figured what did I have to lose? And that is where I got my lucky break. Sarah's manager passed my resume along to the right people within the company and before I knew it I had a position as an intern at Nettwerk. I was so ecstatic that I had been offered an internship, but then reality hit. I was located in Boston and Nettwerk was in California. On top of that, the internship would be unpaid. So I did the only thing I could do if I really wanted to make a future for myself in this industry. I accepted the unpaid position and moved out to Los Angeles, California on my own.

So I started my internship at Nettwerk and immediately fell in love with the job. It was no piece of cake though. I was working roughly 30-35 hours a week at Nettwerk, living in a city where I knew no one, paying to rent an apartment and car, and on top of it having no money coming in. So in order to survive I worked every odd job you could think of around the hours I worked at Nettwerk. I did catering, bartending, valet parking, working as an extra on television shows, and—my personal favorite—a real estate assistant (despite having no license). So in total I was probably working an average of 65 hours a week just so I could have an opportunity to do an unpaid internship in the music industry.

The only reason I was able to make this work for me was because I realized I love this industry and this is what I want to do with my life. Artist management was my calling. There was not one moment when I was working at Nettwerk and felt mad that I was not being paid for the work I did. My days were very busy. I would go into the office and people would already have me "reserved for the day." There were many nights that I would stay at the office later than my supervisor so I could get my work done.

The important thing that I learned about this industry is that if you want to make it you need to be hard-working, perseverant, and personable. I worked with many other interns that I knew half the people in the office did not even know their names. Generally they didn't work more than 10-15 hours per week. I made it a point to come in every morning and say hello to everyone. I wanted my presence to be known. After working at Nettwerk for a couple of months, I started to take matters into my own hands. I would go directly to the managers and ask them personally if there was work that I could do for them. I wanted to prove to them that I was serious about this industry and this company.

I realized that my hard work was paying off when I got an offer to be the assistant to three of the main managers at Nettwerk, including Sarah McLachlan's manager. It was a dream for an intern to even be considered for that position. By accepting the job, though, I would not have been able to finish my degree—an important goal for me. So I decided to return to Boston to finish school early—with the condition that I would have a job at Nettwerk once I graduated. All those hours of interning finally had paid off because now I had the promise of a full-time job that most people spend years trying to get.

So I returned to Boston and overloaded with six courses in order to graduate early. Originally I was a May 2007 graduate and now I will be done by the end of June 2006. Nettwerk luckily has an office in Boston, so I continued interning there. On my one day off, I would go into Nettwerk and work on everything from creating and putting together press kits for artists to developing marketing ideas for tour promotion and CD releases. The best part of this whole co-op experience is that I will be starting full-time with Nettwerk in Boston as an artist manager assistant in July of 2006.

The important lesson that I learned in my co-op experience is that you need to love what you are going to pursue as a career, especially if you want to make it in the entertainment industry. I loved going into work every day even though I wasn't being paid a dime; that was what made me more successful than the other interns. Hard work, determination, and the ability to communicate well with others is also the key to success in this industry. If you can do that, you really can achieve anything you set your mind to.

The Next Theo Epstein

In the previous story, Genevieve alluded to the entertainment world as a "sexy industry." I often talk to my students about what I call Sexy Industry Syndrome, which I define as "any industry that attracts droves of young professionals, with the demand from job hopefuls greatly exceeding the supply of jobs." Examples of "sexy industries" include music industry, TV/film, fashion, advertising, and sports management, among others.

What does it mean if you want to be in a sexy industry? When the demand exceeds the supply of jobs, employers have the luxury of only hiring a very small percentage of candidates... and they also can get away with paying them little or nothing as interns or co-ops. If you don't like it, well, they have plenty of other people willing to accept those terms to get a toehold in that field.

Working in Boston, I meet many young professionals who tell me that their career goal is to be "the next Theo Epstein." At first glance, this makes sense. Epstein is the young, handsome General Manager of baseball's Boston Red Sox—a key architect behind their 2004 World Series championship, the team's first since 1918!

When someone says that they want to be next Theo Epstein, I think they usually have a pretty glamorous vision of what that would entail. They picture watching all the games for free—heck, you're even *paid* to watch the games!—from a luxury box, and it's your job to be obsessed by the sport all day long... as opposed to getting in trouble if you sneak a peak at baseballprospectus.com in many jobs.

My first question for the Theo wannabes is: "Okay, how many hours per week do you think Theo works?" Usually people have no idea. In one *Boston Globe* article from a few years ago, it said that Theo typically worked over 80 hours per week when the team was on the road... and over 100 hours weekly when the team was at home! There was one anecdote about another team's general manager waking up in the middle of the night and calling Theo with a trade idea, figuring Theo would get it first thing in the morning. Instead, Theo picked up the phone in his office... at 2:30 a.m.!

If that's not enough to deter those who are starry-eyed about sports management, I also tell them about a guy I used to know. After getting his MBA, he wanted to go into baseball. He managed to land a job with a team in the lowest level of the minor leagues, out in Idaho. He worked 12-14 hours per day—picking up players at the airport, groundskeeping, you name it, for a few hundred dollars per week—definitely on the bottom of the barrel as far as earnings for someone with an MBA. He did that for a few years but ultimately worked his way up to become the general manager of a Triple-A team—the *highest* level of the minors—in his home state in the southeast.

That's what it takes. Right now I work with a student named Caleb Ginsberg, who is a catcher on Northeastern's baseball team. He is doing everything right and has a difficult but possible dream: He wants to be a bullpen catcher in the major leagues and perhaps become a bullpen coach.

It hasn't been easy. He managed to get some bullpen catcher jobs in the minor league and in the most famous amateur league in the country, the Cape Cod League. He wrote letters to every General Manager in Major League Baseball. Given that he had a very specific goal with some legitimate experience, he actually got a number of calls back from high-profile baseball people. He narrowly missed out on one amazing opportunity but ultimately landed a two-month position with the Tampa Bay Devil Rays, primarily helping that team prepare for the 2006 draft.

On top of all the hard work this is a great guy: someone who is so nice that people want to help him. He's well on his way to making it happen... but it's almost always the hard way when it comes to sexy industries.

A Big Decision

One somewhat amusing aspect of my job is how quickly students transition from one source of anxiety to the next. Quite often, students go into their first professional job search expecting that no one will want to hire them. A few weeks into the job search, many of those same students have a new problem: They have two or three great job offers and are agonizing over which one to accept.

That's what happened to Jaclyn Carron a couple of years ago. The best job she had on her resume was a summer position as a bank teller, but she was smart, sharp, and a great communicator. Sure enough, she ended up with three job offers in short order, and now she was almost in a panic over what to do.

The biggest dilemma was that two of the jobs were in oh-so-familiar Boston, but the *best* job offer was in Atlanta, Georgia. Jaclyn had lived in Massachusetts her whole life and had never been to Georgia. Her parents didn't seem to like the idea of her moving so far away, and Jaclyn herself was daunted by the prospect of having to find a place to live.

"I'm not worried about being able to do the job," she said. "It's just that I'm a really sociable person, and I'm afraid that I'll be so lonely down there, not knowing anyone." Tears welled up in her eyes. "The easiest thing to do would be to accept one of the jobs here," she said. "They aren't bad jobs... It's just that I don't want to be the kind of person who says no to an opportunity just because of being scared."

She took the job in Georgia, and the outcome was surprising. She enjoyed the job and learned a great deal at work, but over time she decided it was not the ideal job for her. However, she found a wonderful roommate and made tons of friends in Atlanta. "Now I *love* the idea of going away for co-op," she said afterwards. By going away, she enjoyed a "double-dip" learning experience, learning on the job while experiencing life beyond Massachusetts without having to make a long-term commitment to leaving New England. Interviewing for her next job, she pursued positions from coast to coast and just started a new job in Manhattan. "I love New York City already," she told me just before this book went to print. Jaclyn certainly conquered her fears of living elsewhere.

The "Float Pool"

For her first co-op, nursing student "Kristin Delvecchio" accepted a position working in the "float pool" for a large health care institution. Working for the float pool is a little like being a temp. You're not assigned to one unit for that health care provider; instead you go to work and they put you where help is needed, anywhere in the facility. Emotionally, it can be a difficult role, as it's very hard to make connections with people due to the fact that you get shuffled around on a regular basis, and you never know quite what to expect.

A month or two into a job she had agreed to hold for six months, Kristin wanted to bail and quit the job, according to Northeastern nursing co-op coordinator Jacki Diani. "I don't know anybody, and nobody knows me," Kristin told Jacki. "I haven't made any friends; I cry every time I get home after work. I need a new job."

Jacki walked through the pros and cons of quitting the job. "First off, you would need to give notice," Jacki told her. "Secondly, if we refer you out for another job at this point, what are you going to say when they ask why you're looking for a job two months into co-op?" Kristin hadn't thought about that. "Then I told her the third option: Stay, and try to make the situation better," Jacki said. "We talked about a fourth scenario: If you make a change and don't like *that* job, then what?

"We also focused on the positives of staying," Jacki added. "By working in the float pool, she was getting exposure to a wide variety of patients: pediatrics, adults, cardiac, gerontology... The job also gave her good pay and a lot of convenience when it came to scheduling."

Kristin decided to meet with the Nurse Manager to discuss how she was feeling. The Nurse Manager was very sympathetic. She emphasized that an effort could be made to have Kristin return to many units over time: She wouldn't have to be a complete stranger every day for six months.

Kristin stuck it out for the six months. The big payoff came during her next job search. "The reaction was, 'Wow, you did six months floating? That's impressive.'" When prospective employers saw her excellent evaluation from her days in the float pool, it said a great deal about her adaptability and perseverance.

Working closely with her co-op coordinator, Kristin also learned how to articulate her float pool experience effectively in interviews. She would talk about how challenging it was and how she benefited greatly from exposure to a wide variety of patients and almost every unit in the hospital! Based on her interviewing skills and that great performance evaluation as a floater, Kristin landed a "plum job" with a well-known, highly regarded specialty hospital, beating out many other candidates in the process.

Hitting The Wall

My former student Michelle George had a terrific first co-op job with a multinational company. Working in an entry-level job in Management Information Systems, Michelle enjoyed ample opportunity to utilize her excellent interpersonal skills and communication skills.

Working with students in computer-related fields, my advice is generally for students to find out just how technical they want to become by "pushing the envelope" to get more and more technical jobs until they find they've reached their limit. That happened for Michelle in a big way—just halfway through her second six-month co-op job.

The position was an electronic commerce job at the same multinational company. Basically, it was using complex computer systems to automate order processing procedures. The role proved to be fiendishly technical. When visiting, I often couldn't make heads or tails of what I overheard when my own students were troubleshooting problems over the phone.

I used to tell students going into that job that this experience would be similar to getting plunked down in China or Russia for six months and having to learn the language from scratch in six months! I would warn them that they likely would feel pretty dumb for the first three months... and then suddenly they would find themselves to be somewhat conversational in this technical jargon, proceeding to increase their fluency all the way through the six-month job.

For most students that effectively described what the job was like. Before Michelle, everyone I knew who worked there ended up loving the job because they never stopped learning. There was always more to know. For Michelle, though, it was different. The job made her feel dumb, alright, but she never really got over that feeling.

It came to a head halfway through her six-month commitment. "I felt a lot of anxiety," she recalls now, seven or eight years after the fact. "I didn't want to go to the office. Time just seemed to slow down, and there were three long months to go. Every single day I had questions. I felt so dumb, and I didn't like that. I was working as hard as I could. When I feel I don't know something, it totally crushes me. And I was not used to feeling that way. I always felt very competent in any job I'd had up to that point."

Despite her anxiety, frustration, and the sinking feeling that the job was just a very bad match for her, Michelle rallied herself by repeating many thoughts to herself: "You have to try to stay positive. Be upbeat. You don't want to burn your bridges. It's not going to be forever; there are only three more months."

She loved her co-workers and focused on the positive energy that she enjoyed from those relationships. "You make connections, and it's easy to underestimate how important those connections are," she recalls. "You meet people, and they keep you going. If you're negative, you're throwing in the towel."

She never gave up, and she earned great respect from everyone by driving herself to do the best she could in spite of the obvious fact that the job wasn't a great match. That turned out to be a key factor in landing a much more suitable job with the same employer. Much to my delight, she ended up as a supervisor in that less technical area where her co-op career had begun, helping my next generation of student employees. She was a huge success on top of being much happier in that role.

3,000 Miles From Home

Years ago my colleague Charlie Bognanni had a student who

accepted a six-month co-op job on the west coast. It was an amazing opportunity, so she accepted it—even though she'd never lived outside of New England.

One month into the job, she called Charlie. She was terribly homesick and wanted to quit and come home. The job was good, but she was so miserable living so far away from loved ones.

Charlie managed to calm her down. He reminded her that she made a commitment for the six months, and that it was important that she keep her word. He urged her to give it more time: After all, it was just a six-month commitment. If she never wanted to return to the far west, she wouldn't have to do so again. It wasn't easy, but she managed to throw herself into her work. She was never truly happy living out there, but she got through the six months and managed to get a very good evaluation in spite of her inner turmoil.

So she returned to Boston, confident that she would never leave the region again. Upon graduation, she got a good job with a local company and prepared to settle in for the long haul in New England.

But then a funny thing happened. She started noticing that her job was kind of boring. She got another job. The same thing eventually happened. She started to appreciate—maybe for the first time—how great that job on the west coast really was. And—much to the amazement of my colleague—she decided to go back to that employer and resigned herself to living 3,000 miles away from Boston.

Many people have some sort of plan for themselves with their career. However, it's important to remember that your priorities will grow and change over time if you remain open to different possibilities. Imagine how much this individual would have missed out on if she gave up on that co-op job when she hit that first hurdle.

The Wrong Career Path
Imagine how hard this would be: For years you've had a dream of being an accountant or an elementary school teacher or civil engineer. You study hard and get good grades throughout college, and you land a great job. Within a few months, though, you come to the horrifying conclusion that you have gone a long way down the wrong career path!

One of the great things about co-ops and internships is that they give you an opportunity to engage in career testing. Maybe you have a 3.8 grade point average in your accounting or education classes, but that only means so much. It's one thing to go to classes in a given subject for a handful of hours each week and then do homework, take tests, and so forth. You may learn whether or not you have the intellectual aptitude in a given field, but will you *like* that field? Will you be happy working long hours during tax season in a busy accounting firm? Can you handle a classroom of 25 fourth-graders? You can't be sure until you do it.

I always feel very sympathetic to the student who returns from co-op and says—usually very sheepishly—"I think what I learned over the last six months is that I'm in the wrong field." Many of these folks think that they will receive an angry response to that statement. Usually I'll want to ask a few questions to make sure it really is the *field* that's the problem—as opposed to a specific organization or type of job within that field—but basically my attitude is "It's great to find that out now."

I have had two students who started in Physical Therapy and graduated as business majors. Both had very solid grades in that challenging field—a solid B+ GPA. Yet through their first real-world experience, they found that working with patients was terribly unsettling for them. Physical therapy is a fairly intimate field in the sense that you need to touch people quite a bit—giving massages, helping them learn stretching and strengthening maneuvers, and so forth. And many of your patients are not exactly young and attractive—some may even have questionable hygiene. If you can't find a way to deal with that professionally, you're in the wrong field.

It's no exaggeration to say that this realization truly shook up these two students: It affected their very identity. It took some courage to realize that they were on the wrong road, given the hassle and expense of switching programs. But it doesn't matter how much you know about a field or how great the job market is in that area if you're not going to be comfortable going to work every day.

Double Trouble?

Some young professionals are quick to focus on the thorns in their first jobs, while others emerge from even the toughest situations smelling like a rose. Mary Rose Tichar, Director of the Cooperative Education Program at Case Western Reserve, passed along this true story of a student who had ample reason to fail at both *of her co-ops: Saddled with low-level work at her first job and frustrating developments on her second job, she didn't let these issues sidetrack her career progression. It's a concise but effective example of how seeing the big picture sometimes requires persistence in the face of new forms of adversity.*

The first co-op for chemical engineering student "Lorraine Sanderson" was a disappointment. She did not do a lot of work relevant to being a chemical engineer. Her positive outlook and attitude carried her through, and she left the co-op with good relationships and with plenty of respect.

Lorraine's second co-op was perfect—or so it seemed. She worked at a pharmaceutical company—a perfect fit for her long term goals. She moved, set up a new apartment, and dug in. Then the company faced some difficult challenges with the efficacy of some drugs and began to make sweeping changes. The other students at this company wrote me e-mails about how disappointed and discouraged they felt. Not Lorraine. Again, her cheerful attitude kept her going and with great diplomacy—her natural talent—she developed relationships. With some effort, she found that her supervisor was a good listener, and Lorraine communicated with her regularly to make sure her boss was aware of her interests and goals. She also offered to help with projects outside of her immediate responsibility.

Soon she was asked to help on some challenging lab projects. Ultimately she came back to campus with a huge smile on her face! In her senior year, she was offered a full-time job with a top pharmaceutical company and Lorraine says she never would have gotten this job without her co-op at the pharmaceutical company.

A Knight Of The Roundtable

On his first co-op, Greg Fischer worked in a sales and marketing role for a financial information provider in downtown Boston. It was a small enough place that the company president would run a regular "roundtable" discussion for all employees. "How's everyone doing?" the president would ask. "Are there any concerns? Are there things that we could be doing better?"

Greg noticed that not many people participated in these meetings—especially the youngest and newest professionals like himself. He decided that he was going to make an effort to participate. Paying more attention to the company's processes and policies, he began finding opportunities for change and voicing them at the roundtables in a positive, solution-oriented way.

On top of receiving support for many of his suggestions, Greg found that his behavior led to him being pegged as a guy who could think about the big picture beyond his somewhat low-level duties. Ultimately he was asked to fill in for senior salespeople when they left—even though he was a first-time co-op!

It's absolutely amazing how many people just do their jobs without ever stopping to wonder if there are better ways to do things. Many long-time employees cannot really identify how their role fits into the overall mission of the organization. If you can't understand why your job matters or figure out better ways to do your job, it is much more difficult to elevate yourself in any organization. Speak up, ask questions, and get interested in why your job matters and how your group's role fits into the mission of the company. What you learn may change your approach to work dramatically.

The Big Layoff

Amy Black, NU Class of 2000, obtained one of our most glamorous co-op jobs back in the late 1990s. She worked out of state in a popular vacation destination for good pay with a world-famous consulting company. They even provided free housing, free flights, and shared use of a free rental car! All of her friends were envious about this near-fantasy experience.

However, that scenario went sour before she completed her six months. Due to a merger, her employer ended up laying off 25 percent of the employees at Amy's site. Her manager was a key decision-maker, so she heard many chilling details about the planned layoff. In particular, management was concerned because of a story that was in the news at the time. A disgruntled employee at another "household name" corporation had "gone postal." After being terminated, he went on a rampage. He owned several guns and ended up shooting and killing several former co-workers.

The management at Amy's employer did some quick research and found that about half of their workforce had gun permits—many had gun racks on the roofs of their cars! The managers decided to bring in a security firm to handle the terminations, but no one explained to Amy how that was going to work... or suggested that she should just stay home that day.

So the following Monday, Amy overheard an intense voice near her work area. It was a man she didn't know saying "Julie, get up... and step away from your desk!" In a panic, Amy jumped under her desk, not sure what was going on. Eventually her boss saw her there in tears and apologized for not handling the situation with her more appropriately.

Amy looks back and laughs at her panic now, but the experience still has had an impact on her to this day. "The takeaway from this for me was 'Always have your resume ready and updated: You never know what might happen; your job is never secure.'"

Another lesson from this one is that it's *always* in your best interest to make yourself indispensable in a job as opposed to someone who just gets by. If your employer does need to downsize, you certainly want to be on a list of employees that they can't do without, if at all possible. That won't guarantee that you won't ever be laid off or let go, but it's gives you the best opportunity possible to leave a job on your own terms.

Pioneer Engineer

Several years ago Microsoft decided to hire a student for a position in Reno, Nevada for the first time. Kristin Poole was an Industrial Engineering student, and her coordinator and I thought she was an excellent person for an excellent job.

The only question in accepting the job was the fact that it was in Reno and that she would be the only co-op there. Furthermore, while our other co-ops with the company would be able to live in company-provided housing or together in apartments near Microsoft's headquarters in Redmond, Washington, there naturally was no similar situation in Reno. Linda would have to live in a hotel near the Microsoft campus for the six months.

We talked for a long while about the decision. One thing we kept coming back to was what a great story it would be for her in the future. She would be a pioneer for Northeastern—our first co-op in Reno, Nevada. It would say so much about her flexibility and her willingness to make sacrifices with the long run in mind.

She accepted the job and proved to be a superstar. She earned so much respect from high-level people in the corporate headquarters. "Somehow she's managed to stay more connected to us up here than some of the interns who actually work right here on campus!" I heard.

Kristin continued to explore on her third co-op, once again pushing the envelope by trying something totally different once again: a finance co-op position in Boston. But when she graduated, it was far from "out of sight, out of mind" at Microsoft. They lured her back for a lucrative and exciting position upon graduation.

A "Sexy" Job

Chris Wright, Northeastern University Class of 2000, talked to me recently about his co-op days in the late 1990s. Growing up in Saugus, Massachusetts—just a short drive from our campus—Chris had never really gone far from home in his life.

That changed when he got a co-op job several hours from home and had to relocate for the co-op. As a life experience, Chris recalls that he was nervous and scared but also excited about living and working far from home. Better still, the job appeared to be a dream come true. Chris would be working in sports marketing. "It was what I always thought I wanted to do," he says.

Chris worked on promotions for this firm. In many ways, the job was not different from others he had had. He did research on the Internet and worked with a large client on special promotions. There also was a travel element, which seemed exciting.

Soon, though, Chris found that his role was not as glamorous as he had imagined it to be. Working on promotions in sports marketing can be unbelievably time-intensive. When working an event, a 20-hour day was generally the rule. And all co-ops and interns were paid on a salary basis—just as they would be if they were full-time employees. "One intern from another school told me she figured she was really making something like $1 an hour," Chris recalls. "I think she might have been exaggerating, but she definitely was working 15 to 20 hours a day, seven days a week."

On the whole, Chris now says, "It was a great experience but also eye-opening. It was a strain."

In the end, there were a few takeaway lessons for Chris. While surprised to learn that "just going away for six months wasn't all that bad," he adds that "Those 'sexy' jobs aren't necessarily all that great."

This is consistent with what I hear from many young professionals. I know one young woman who is trying to break into a behind-the-scenes career in pro hockey, and says, "People think that they're going to make tons of money if they make it, but the truth is you don't really make that much money... so you'd *better* love it!"

Dead Last

At Northeastern, we require all first-time co-ops to take a class called COPU101, Professional Development for Co-op. Often we have a mix of students in the class—sometimes our co-op faculty members get to instruct their own advisees, sometimes not. "Tricia Hartigan" was in my class, and she also was my advisee. So things were teed up for her to have an opportunity to learn how to write resumes, interview, and so forth while also having the chance to show me that she deserved to be sent to some of my best employers.

Initially, it didn't work out that way. It was a one-credit class that met for just one hour each week, but Tricia had trouble getting there on time and in completing the modest homework assignments. It just seemed like the class was not a priority to her.

The low point came when she e-mailed me the day AFTER an assignment was due to ask me if I could forward it to her again and also explain it to her because she hadn't really understood it to begin with.

I decided the time had come for some unemotional but intense honesty. "You have a 3.6 GPA, so you're obviously a smart person," I told her. "However, if I had to rank this class in terms of performance to date, right now I would rank you dead last of 37 students."

Initially she was stunned. She mumbled something about how she couldn't imagine that things were really that bad. I enumerated her various minor and major transgressions, and then said, "If you can't get to my class on time or let me know in advance of a deadline when you're having difficulty with an assigned task, why should I believe that you're suddenly going to be able to rise to the occasion when you're working in a job that you obtain through me? How can I possibly recommend you to one of my employers and feel confident that you'll reflect positively on me?"

Suddenly the light bulb went on. I wasn't looking for a teacher-student relationship; I wanted a supervisor-employee relationship. From that day on, Tricia did a great job, and we still have a great relationship. After completing co-op successfully and doing a great job on her second search, I said to her, "It's hard to believe now that you had such a difficult time for that first month in my class."

She laughed. "I was just immature," she said. "I don't think I was emotionally ready for co-op." I generally don't think of maturity as something that one can develop in a hurry, but it happened with her.

"On Co-op for 27 Years"

For a decade, Sean Jones was best known as a formidable defensive lineman in the National Football League. He played for the Los Angeles Raiders, Houston Oilers, and Green Bay Packers, and earned an invitation to the Pro Bowl in 1993. He ended his career as a professional athlete with a flourish, starting at defensive end for the Packers and becoming a first-time Super Bowl champion in his very last game.

Well before that pinnacle, though, Sean already had earned a reputation as a superstar in the workplace. He attended Northeastern University many years before I arrived on the scene, but my retired colleague Mike Ablove used to rave about Sean's job performance. So when it came time to put together some compelling stories for this book, I decided to track him down.

Like many promising athletes, Sean had numerous options when it came to selecting a university. Rather than focusing solely on sports, he quickly developed an appreciation for other elements in that decision. "What differentiated Northeastern from other fine schools was that it gave you the opportunity to get real-world experience," Sean says. "Once I got there, I was encouraged. It was something I saw that was tangible. I saw other people having success. You were brought into a program where that was expected. If you were in the business school, you had to have a co-op. You had to find a way to make sure it was meaningful. It was less of my doing and more the curriculum that was set up at Northeastern."

Despite his athletic gifts, Sean's feet were firmly on the ground when it came to setting priorities as a college student. "You have to take advantage of where you are now because you don't know where you're going to be. I didn't want to take the chance and just bet everything on being a professional athlete. Because the reality was that it was like buying a lottery ticket—a lottery ticket versus cash.

"I knew I had cash in my pocket because of Northeastern. I had the mindset that if I did not play football after Northeastern—which was very realistic—then I had a good job. I had a chance to grow and develop and keep going."

Even as a first-time co-op, Sean had a powerful learning experience. "I co-oped at F.W. Woolworth in New York City," he recalls. "I remember the first thing I was required to do. I had to help put together a system where they consolidated all the different stores and the different assets. At the time they were all individual and at the end of the year they had to go through this painstaking task of putting it all together. So we created a computer system that was programmed to download their information directly and consolidate it at one point so each month you could look at it. You wouldn't think it would be so antiquated in 1981, '82, but it just shows technology-wise how much business has changed.

"Just being able to go through that and dealing with people who were so passionate about what they were doing and how this implementation was really going to affect how Woolworth did business, you couldn't help but fall in line and be passionate about it, too. It was not so much being passionate about computers and spreadsheets—I don't know how you do that; I'm not a computer geek—it was more about the workplace itself and how people came to work every day and saw a goal and were focused on what they wanted to get done. It made me understand that there are very, very good people out there. It's like sports: If you want to be good at it, you have to work at it."

It's no exaggeration to say his first experience in a corporate environment completely transformed his expectations about the world of work. "You have this idea that work is this painstaking thing where you get up in the morning, get a cup of coffee, jump on a train, and go to work—just bide your time, and at 5 o'clock you're off. In other words, you're just working to get paid.

"I think that's what a lot of people end up doing, but what I saw working at a F.W. Woolworth was how important it was for people to realize what they need to do to win. For us to win, we need a game plan; we need to execute. That's where the analogy is between sports and business. Once I saw it in that regard, it was no different than attacking a game plan or going after it as we did with football games. There are a lot of similarities."

Surviving and succeeding for ten years as a defensive lineman in the National Football League is no easy feat. I asked Sean if he thought that his remarkable longevity was connected to the work ethic he had developed as a co-op student. His answer surprised me as much as it pleased me.

"I think my longevity came from the fact that it wasn't the only thing I did," he says now. "While people were wearing their bodies out in the 'off-season' and thought they had to do that, I always had other things to do. I was always working, so I didn't beat up on myself, and my mind was fresh when I started the season again. I could focus back on football.... I always looked at football as school and the off-season as co-op. I've been on co-op for 27 years!"

Even after he had made it as a professional athlete, Sean continued to advance his corporate career. "I always had it so if I ever wanted to go back to Woolworth, I could. Every year I played, the job got better because they also saw me having more experience, and I was more beneficial for the company as I got older. So they saw me as an asset, and they really invested time in me. It was always good to know I had something to fall back on."

Woolworth kept him on for several years, and his time in the

Big Apple piqued his interest in the stock market. He ended up working as a stockbroker for Dean Witter for nine years, started his own business, and worked with charitable foundations. He still does brokerage work on top of having a role as an executive for the Raiders, assisting them with personnel decisions.

"I don't think any job is job-specific," he says. "It's like the old Shakespeare adage that the whole world is a stage and we're just playing the part. No matter where you work, they're all the same jobs. It's a matter of applying what you already know to that new job. It's not a football job; it's not a finance job: It's work, and it requires managing people and developing people or products. It's all the same thing.

"With regard to football, the product is entertainment, and we're trying to get the best players to help entertain the fans—no different than if you work for Eastman Kodak. You're still trying to get the best line, the best product, so people enjoy what you do. That's what I do in a nutshell. I'm a personnel executive for the team. I try to bring bodies and get the best players in the room to make sure we can compete."

Today at Northeastern, I work with many athletes, and quite a few of them are able to transfer their ability to work in a team and leadership skills into an organizational setting. Most recently I have enjoyed working with Lauren Edelmeier, an All-American field hockey player who is also a superstar in the classroom and workplace. During tax season as an accounting co-op, she literally raced back and forth repeatedly from the office to the playing field one Saturday to compete in a tournament while ensuring she met her employer's needs during crunch time.

Sometimes, though, I work with students who struggle to focus significant energy on anything outside of their sport, whether it's a varsity or club activity. I like to tell these students the story of Sean Jones, whose career has shown that it's entirely possible to be successful at the highest level as an athlete—without forgetting to plan for the many years after the cheering has come to an end.

A Co-op Odyssey

Back in January 1974, Northeastern University MBA student Bill Sloane was preparing for his second academic quarter and his first co-op experience. He got a call from the Director of MBA Co-op Placement about a possible job, but it didn't sound too exciting. A school was looking for someone who could do a feasibility study about adding an Associate Degree program. Bill had teaching experience and seemed to be a plausible candidate, but the job had "no particular appeal" until the Director mentioned that the school was in northern Greece. "I'll be right over!" Bill said.

Making it happen required some sacrifices. "After interviewing, being offered and accepting the job, I dropped coursework, sublet my apartment, rented a truck to move belongings back home to Newburyport, and took a series of Greek lessons from a musician who had worked with folk singer Joan Baez," Bill recalls.

Before he knew it, Bill was immersed in meeting with educators in Greece, working on curricular and operational elements related to the project. "With limited knowledge of Greek and modern Greek culture, and with only one quarter of business studies completed at Northeastern, I did my best to gather relevant data and develop it into a rough proposal for the President's use in discussion with the Trustees," Bill says.

The pay was $125/month—pretty modest even for 1975. But he had a top-floor apartment with a stunning view of the Aegean Sea and Mount Olympos, the inspiration for myths that have been told for eons. "The joy I felt at my good fortune was boundless," Bill recalls. "Students who have returned to studies at NU from work abroad uniformly voice the same thought that for them it has been not just a 'work' experience; it has been a 'life' experience. This was true for me as well."

One highlight was a ski trip to a Yugoslavian village called Skopje—now part of Macedonia. "We arrived late on a Friday night and checked into a large A-frame chalet inn, the only available accommodation in the village," Bill says. "When we awoke the next morning and looked out to the parking lot, ours was the only car there! After waiting for some time, we inquired about the timing of the start of the lift. Vague verbal responses and gestures at the clock left us puzzled.

"Then, the bus from the city arrived. The place sprang to life! People poured from the bus, Slavic music began to fill the air from speakers mounted high on lift towers, and a large circle formed as people danced their joy. People with and without skis rode the lift to the top; the skiers skied down, those without skis walked around the spacious hilltop and re-boarded the lift to the bottom. For about $1.25, we skied all day."

Over the months that followed, Bill enjoyed the wondrous ruins of Athens, the wildflowers and olive trees of Crete, and a bus trip to see treasures of the Ottoman Empire in Istanbul. The odyssey culminated in a two-day hike up Mount Olympos. For icing on the cake, his co-op included side trips to France and Italy, including a sailing trip to Corsica and Sardinia that provided him with a good excuse to delay his journey back to the States.

The trip proved to be the turning point in Bill's life and career. As a true believer in the co-op model of personal and professional development, Bill obtained a position on our co-op faculty on November 17, 1975.

That particular odyssey just came to an end in June 2006 after a remarkable remarkable 30 years in cooperative education. None of it would have happened if he'd hadn't been ready and willing when the opportunity knocked and a door opened where he hadn't known one existed.

CHAPTER SIX

Control What You Can

The most difficult time I've faced in my current job as a co-op coordinator had nothing to do with working with students or employers. This happened many years ago now. When I first came to Northeastern back in March 1995, all of the cooperative education faculty had offices in one building. The business co-op coordinators were together on one floor.

Most of us liked it that way. Surrounded by professionals engaged in the same work, it was easy to get advice and assistance when needed... or to get together for lunch. Sometimes our students needed to work with more than one coordinator—perhaps a marketing student was considering a job in finance, for example. The close proximity of our offices made those "cross-referrals" relatively easy.

A few years later, though, the university decided that it would be best to "relocate" all of the co-op coordinators to their respective colleges. In other words, the powers-that-be saw more value in having the co-op faculty rub shoulders with our academic counterparts instead of with each other. The hope was that this would facilitate greater integration between co-op and the classroom.

While this was an admirable goal, most of the co-op faculty believed that what we would gain would not offset what we would lose by splitting up the co-op faculty. Space was also an issue: Some colleges had ample room to provide co-op coordinators with good offices close to the academic faculty, while this posed significant challenges in other programs. Several of my colleagues were so angry about this development that they ultimately quit their jobs.

I was frustrated, too. I was in a suite that was across the hall from the Management Information Systems academic faculty. In my immediate suite, there were a handful of full-time statistics professors and then several offices shared by statistics TAs and part-timers. Depending on the day or the time of year, I might be the only one in the suite—some days I would unlock the suite and work all day without seeing a soul, and then lock it up at night. I'm not exactly a social butterfly at work, but I felt isolated.

There were times when I wondered if I, too, should look for another job. Then the turning point came, and it was more of a change within my outlook rather than any external event that happened.

I had to accept that, like it or not, there were many things I could not control about my current job circumstances. The University had made a decision, and my options were to leave or to live with it as best I could. I resolved that I would make an effort to put less energy into what I could not control and more effort into the things I could control.

I decided that I would focus on making my very small corner of the university as positive and productive as I could. Handling one of the largest loads of students at the time, I had an opportunity to hire some support in my immediate area. I decided that it would be critical to not only hire people who could do the tasks at hand: They would need to be people who would make me look forward to coming into that suite every day.

I received authorization to hire some temporary help to get me through the semester. I reached out to my friend Susan Bacher who knew nothing about co-op, but she had great interpersonal skills and whose background was such that she could master what needed to be done quickly. She also would be a great addition in terms of building a positive atmosphere—having known her for years, I had no doubt about that.

Then I hired a graduate student. I interviewed some candidates from our MBA program who had the advantage of knowing the functional aspects of business. But in interviewing them I was not impressed with them interpersonally. Would they be people who had the sensitivity to critique resumes and practice interviews? Were they people I wanted to train and mentor? Not really.

Subsequently I interviewed Jessica Rossier, a Mexican graduate student in our Counseling Psychology program. What an amazing person! We had a great and candid discussion: She was completely confident that she could handle practice interviews but cautioned me that her English might make it difficult for her to catch subtle errors on a resume. I wasn't worried about that: I needed her to overhaul resumes; I could handle the fine-tuning.

Even though neither person worked full-time hours, both decisions turned out to be among the best I've ever made. Susan was fantastic with students, and her positive energy gave me a much-needed boost. Jessica was amazing as well—great with interviewing, far better than either of us expected on the resumes, and always willing to contribute any way she could without complaint. She also tipped me off to another great grad student, Daniela Diaz, an engineering student from Venezuela. She had the same strengths as Jessica, and my numbers kept growing. We hired her as well... and a few years later these relationships led to hiring a third great grad assistant, Nayeli Vivanco. I ended up getting four or five years' worth of assistance all stemming from that one hire!

Within a matter of a few months, the experience of coming into the suite every day changed dramatically for me. I no longer felt isolated: I had a very small but terrific team of professionals in place. I also found ways to get together with my counterparts on the co-op faculty through lunches and other informal get-togethers. It was more of an effort as the situation no longer made spontaneous interaction a frequent occurrence, but it could be done.

When we had several openings on the business co-op faculty, I volunteered to chair the search committee and was able to have a major role in ensuring that those new hires would be great colleagues as well as great professionals for our students and employers.

I also befriended Sangit Chatterjee, one of the stats professors in my suite, a brilliant man with many eclectic interests. We ended up co-authoring one of the most ambitious pieces of writing I've ever attempted—a journal article that we hoped would unite the fields of sports, evolutionary biology, philosophy, and statistics. Getting to know him has added to my appreciation of my work environment.

Few professionals are likely to agree with every move that is made by their organization. Sometimes changes have such a negative impact that it is indeed necessary to move on to a new employer. First, though, it's vital to see what can be accomplished by worrying about what you *can* control instead of obsessing about what you can't.

The Sixth Key – Control What You Can

The sixth key to professional success is to control what you can. Author and editor Arthur Gordon said:

"Some people confuse acceptance with apathy, but there's all the difference in the world. Apathy fails to distinguish between what can and what cannot be helped; acceptance makes that distinction. Apathy paralyzes the will-to-action; acceptance frees it by relieving it of impossible burdens."

Philosopher, teacher, and author Ralph Waldo Trine said:

"To get up each morning with the resolve to be happy... is to set our own conditions to the events of each day. To do this is to condition circumstances instead of being conditioned by them."

Back in 1942, a member of Alcoholics Anonymous came across the following words in a *New York Herald Tribune* obituary:

"God grant us the serenity to accept the things we cannot change, courage to change the things we can, and wisdom to know the difference."

In some form or another, those words may have come down from the Greeks or Roman or any of a number of possible sources: No one is sure. However, that prayer has become a cornerstone of the Alcoholics Anonymous philosophy. But you certainly don't need to be an alcoholic or even remotely religious to understand the power of that statement.

In your career—or in life in general—difficult things are going to happen. So why waste energy on what can't be changed, regardless of how much you turn it over in your mind? Conversely, just because it's possible to make changes doesn't mean that it's easy—it can take an effort of will. And knowing what can and cannot be changed is probably the most difficult task of all. Sometimes you have to go forward *as if* something is within your control, even when you're not sure whether it truly is.

This concept comes up all the time in my line of work. While anxiously preparing for interviews, students often have a few questions that make me smile: "How many people are applying for this job? Do other candidates have more experience than me? Do I have the highest grade point average of the candidates? Will this employer think my computer skills are good enough for this job?"

I usually just shrug and smile when I get these questions. If people push harder for me to answer them, I usually say something like this. "Don't spin your wheels expending energy on things that you can't control. With any interview, your best bet is to assume that you're up against several terrific candidates and that it will take your best efforts to get the offer. Why would you ever not make that assumption?

"Likewise, you might have the most or least experience or the highest or lowest grade point average of any candidate. Regardless, it is what is, and there's nothing you can to do change those factors at this point in the process.

"So worry about what you *can* control. You can out-prepare the competition—usually that's not even that hard to do. Maybe you can't learn a new software application in a day or two, but you *can* read up on it so you can have an intelligent conversation with the employer instead of repeatedly reciting 'I don't know anything about it, but I'm willing to learn.'"

The same applies once you are in a job. You seldom can have an impact on organizational strategies and policies, and you may not even have much of a say in terms of what your day-to-day responsibilities might be. You generally can't choose who you work with early in your career. But you *can* do whatever you're asked to do to the best of your ability, and you can be ready to change how you approach your job or handle various tasks based on how open you are to coaching and criticism.

Working requires considerable energy. Don't waste that energy on things that are out of your control; use it where that effort will make a difference.

Elements of Controlling What You Can

Reflecting on many stories featuring themes related to controlling what you can, I discovered numerous elements that comprise this key to professional success:

1. Live in the moment.
Some of the unhappiest people that you will meet in the workplace are those who either dwell on the past or the future. While you don't want to forget what you have learned from all that has transpired in your past, you need to get over bad feelings and not be consumed by them. Likewise, you can't let past mistakes or failures paralyze you when the opportunity arises for a second chance. Lastly, don't make one common mistake that young professionals sometimes make: Focus on doing well on the tasks at hand instead of spending time and energy dreaming or scheming of better work in the future. If you don't do well in the here and now, you won't have a better future.

2. Be coachable.
Several years ago, there was a National Football League player named Bobby Grier. His son Mike took up hockey and ended up at Boston University. On the one hand, he had great upside, but entering college he was overweight and too slow on his skates. So as a former professional athlete, what did Bobby Grier ask of his son as he went off to play Division I college hockey? It wasn't to score a ton of goals or to lose weight or to become a star. It was

simply this: "Be coachable." Mike Grier did just that, and he is now a solid player in the National Hockey League.

I thought that was a great message. Especially in the highly competitive field of athletics, very few can make it to the highest level. Success is not guaranteed, and an injury can end a career in a heartbeat. So what more can you do except to give the advice of being coachable? If you are coachable—meaning that you are open to getting constructive criticism and acting on it—then it probably will result in a great effort. And if you do everything right and still don't make it as an athlete, you can feel good about yourself—whatever the outcome.

The same is true in the workplace. The best professionals are not defensive or dismissive when someone makes a suggestion that will help them improve. When you're open in this way, personal and professional growth are almost inevitable.

3. Seek out criticism.

I'll take it one step further. Even if you're open to criticism, you may not get enough of it unless you ask for it. A great manager will give you great feedback regularly, but a great employee will ask for it if it's not forthcoming. And the best employees won't just write off a negative evaluation or blame their supervisor for it: They'll do everything in their power to figure out what role they played in getting that disappointing result.

4. Learn from mistakes.

It's basically impossible to avoid making mistakes. Obviously you want to do as much as you can to prevent mistakes from happening, but how you respond when they do occur will have a big impact on how you are perceived by managers, co-workers, and even customers. Can you own responsibility for mistakes and focus on solutions instead of finger-pointing? Can you scrutinize your mistakes to understand why they happened and then grow as a result?

Malcolm Gladwell, best-selling author of *The Tipping Point* and *Blink*, wrote a terrific article for *The New Yorker* on "physical genius." He tried to capture what it was that separated great performers from ordinary ones in fields such as sports, classical music, and brain surgery. For me, the most memorable moment of the piece came when Gladwell talked to someone who interviewed brain surgeons.

This individual had found a fascinating difference between the top brain surgeons and the ones who were not at that level. In the interview, he found that the one crucial question was to ask about mistakes that the surgeons had made. Almost invariably, the so-so performers would say that they did not make mistakes. Meanwhile, the exceptional surgeons would talk with great energy about really interesting mistakes they had made and what they had learned from them to become better at dealing with the multitude of scenarios that arise.

That kind of passion to dissect performance and learn from it is something that differentiates great professionals from those content to be pretty good.

True Stories about Controlling What You Can

The Right Direction

"Pamela" was one of my many Chinese-born students—the older sister, in fact, of "Eddie," the young man you read about earlier in this book who was the very last student to get a job the first time he looked for one. Having immigrated to the United States as a teenager, Pamela felt self-conscious about her heavy Chinese accent and generally overwhelmed thinking about going out to interview for her first professional job.

We talked about all the things that made her nervous and broke them down into things that she *can* control and things that she *can't* control. There were plenty in that second category: She was afraid that her English would keep her from getting jobs, and that was a definite possibility. She wasn't sure if her computer skills were good enough to get a job in Information Technology, and she was worried that there might be other candidates who were stronger than she was.

Although these anxieties were entirely legitimate, I explained to her that it was useless wasting energy on things she couldn't change. We worked on crafting an answer to an anticipated question on weaknesses, so she could talk about her hard work on improving her English. But fundamentally we couldn't change her ability to speak and be understood, nor could we do much about her current technical skill level. As for the competition from other job seekers, I encouraged her to always expect that she was up against good candidates: This might motivate her to prepare more diligently.

Fortunately, there were a few things that Pamela could control. She worried about not being prepared for the interview, and I assured her that she certainly could outwork any other candidate in that area if she chose to do so. The probability of sweaty palms worried her, so we devised a few subtle ways in which she could dry them shortly before that initial handshake.

Lastly, she was very anxious about getting lost and being late to the interview, given that she was relatively knew to the Boston area. Her first interview was coming up in a few days at MIT Lincoln Laboratory, located about a half-hour northwest of Boston in Lexington, Massachusetts. Not really thinking she would agree to it, I still encouraged her to drive out to the company a day in advance so she would know exactly where she was going.

You can't imagine my surprise at the phone call I got the day before her interview. Calling from her cellphone, Pamela said, "Mr. Weighart, it's Pamela! I tried to drive to the company with my brother, but we missed the turn onto I-95. We're in New

Hampshire!"

It didn't seem like a promising omen for this interview. I explained where they had gone wrong, and she called later to tell me that they had found their way to the company. "That's great," I said. "Now tomorrow, here's what I want you to do: Odds are that when they meet you in the lobby, they'll ask you if you had any trouble finding the place. Now, I don't think you need to tell them about your wrong turn and going to New Hampshire. Instead, just say, 'No: I drove out yesterday to make sure I would have no trouble being on time today.'"

Naturally, they were impressed. Instead of dreading that first sweaty handshake, Pamela found that she had reason to feel confident she would make a great first impression. They offered her a job, and she did both of her co-ops with the Lab.

A Bad Evaluation

My co-op colleagues Jacki Diani and Mary Carney passed along this instructive tale about one of their nursing students. "Nancy Ivers" worked for a large, well-respected Boston-area hospital for her first co-op. It's a typical first job for many Northeastern students: The position involved adult in-patient care. Many nursing students often yearn to work with children in some more exciting settings, but this job can be a useful "stepping-stone" position on that career path. Some students adjust easily to the adult in-patient role, while others have struggled.

Nancy had touched base with Jacki via e-mail halfway through the co-op to indicate that everything was fine, so it was a surprise when Nancy showed up in tears on Jacki's doorstep very soon after she completed the job. Much to Nancy's shock and dismay, she had received a bad evaluation from the Nurse Supervisor.

Her evaluator hadn't held back. The evaluation detailed how Nancy had failed to take initiative; she commented "Did the minimum to complete tasks." The supervisor felt she was lazy and uninterested in work and that she wasn't putting in any extra effort. The evaluation read: "Seems distracted, indifferent, focused on breaks, not well integrated on the unit... Not on the unit looking for work to do or to helps others." Most upsetting was a comment the supervisor made on the phone when Jacki called to follow up about the evaluation: The supervisor questioned whether Nancy was really cut out for nursing or not.

Obviously, it would have been better if Nancy had been more proactive and sought out feedback much earlier during her work term: She had contacted Jacki and told her that all was well, but that was based solely on her own perceptions instead of through communication with her supervisor. Now that bad evaluation was out of her control: Nothing could change the fact that it existed. But Jacki gave her credit for facing up to the evaluation by coming in to discuss it right after she received it.

During their discussion, Nancy said she felt that the evaluation wasn't fair: She *did* do her job well. She and her supervisor was rarely even on the same floor: How would she know whether her performance was good or not, anyway?

Jacki told her that the supervisor likely got input from other managers and full-time nurses in the area. She also acknowledged that it was indeed possible that the evaluation was not fair. However, "right or wrong, this is her impression," Jacki told Nancy.

Working together, they dug deeper into what had happened during the job. "I was nervous," Nancy admitted, describing what it was like to work for the first time with real patients with real problems alongside very busy health care professionals. "I felt intimidated by the staff."

Jacki asked her to write a reflection paper in which she could try to make sense of what she had learned from the job, the work environment, and the negative evaluation. Nancy agreed to do it. Then she also added that not only was she convinced that nursing was still right for her, she actually wanted to interview at one of the most competitive employers for the next cycle.

"You know, they likely are going to ask to see your evaluation from this job," Jacki told her. Nancy got upset all over again. Jacki laid out her options. "Well, you could lie and say you never got an evaluation, but I wouldn't recommend that," Jacki said. "I would recommend being candid in the interview–tell them you want to talk about your evaluation. And then you could follow up by giving them the reflection paper, so you can show them what you learned about yourself through that tough first experience."

Nancy e-mailed her reflection paper to Jacki. It was adequate–about a page, not too deep, but it touched on a few key points.

About a month later, Nancy interviewed for that very competitive position. Afterward, she followed up with her coordinator. "I did everything you said," Nancy told Jacki. "Everything went great."

Jacki was somewhat skeptical until she found out that Nancy had decided that her reflection paper really didn't cut it. She rewrote it and probed much deeper into examining what went wrong. She took responsibility for much of what went wrong. She even seemed to have a better appreciation of the Nurse Supervisor's perspective. That manager was swamped! Suddenly the light had come on: It wasn't all about her. She developed more respect for the challenges of that setting and obviously had grown a great deal through what had happened. She talked about her need to be more proactive about obtaining feedback.

To Jacki's amazement, Nancy got that next job she wanted. But only after she had taken a bad evaluation, dissected it, learned from it, and "turned it upside down."

If At First...
"Wardell Scott" didn't exactly get off on the right foot when he began his co-op career. The first time he came to see me, it was mid-June. "I want to get a co-op job," he told me.

"For January?" I asked.

"Uh, no," he said. "For now."

He wanted a co-op that would begin in two weeks despite being two months late to look for a job. And it's not as if we're a placement office: He would need to buy my co-op textbook, use it to prepare a resume, get that critiqued, and then prep for and complete a practice interview successfully.

I was skeptical about how it would turn out and told him so. "We can give it a try, but you've put yourself in a real hole by waiting so long to get started."

His practice interview was okay except for one significant mistake at the end. When asked if he had any questions, he had only one: "How much does this job pay?"

Afterwards, I explained to him why that was not a great question to ask. Employers would have a problem with that: It sent the message that the money was all that interested him.

At last he went on his first interview. I called the employer for feedback and learned he would not be offered the job. "We were kind of turned off because the only question he asked was how much the job paid," the interviewer said.

I don't get angry too often with students, but I don't have much patience with someone who makes the same mistake twice after being given constructive and thorough feedback about that mistake. I called up Wardell. "Remember I told you that it would be a problem if you asked a question about pay?" I said. "Well, guess what? You asked a question about pay, and it was a problem!"

Wardell ended up getting a mediocre job that time—a direct result of his late start in what was actually a strong job market at the time. To his credit, though, he learned from his mistake. When things don't go well for some students, they start to assume that the co-op program is the problem. Wardell knew that he had blown it, and he improved greatly in terms of coachability from then on.

He got great jobs for his second and third co-op, and he ultimately became one of my top choices when bringing in upperclassmen to talk to freshmen and sophomores about the lessons they had learned. Wardell would tell his story, always starting off by saying, "First of all, don't do what I did!"

Lessons in Preparation

As a paid hobby of sorts, I write for www.uscho.com, also known as US College Hockey Online. Over the last six years or so, I've covered dozens of games and interviewed countless players and coaches.

One of my favorite stories from this experience involved a post-game interview with Boston University hockey coach Jack Parker. As of this writing, Parker is has the fourth-most coaching victories in college hockey history with 715 wins over a 33-year career behind the bench. He is also a blunt expert when it comes to a post-game post-mortem.

After one loss a few years ago, Parker told the press corps, "It was obvious before we went out on the ice that we weren't prepared to play. I looked around the locker room, and it seemed like no one wanted to be there. And it showed in how we played out there in the first period."

One scribe posed a question for the veteran coach. "What did you do between the first and second periods to deal with the fact that the team wasn't prepared to play tonight?"

Parker looked baffled, momentarily. "Nothing," he said. "The time to be prepared had come and gone at that point."

I told this story to a student back in April 2006. "Zeke Isaacson" had interviewed for a job with a Supply Chain Management employer. Going into the interview, he wasn't sure how he felt about the job, so he didn't prepare all that much. Over the course of a lengthy interview with the charismatic entrepreneur, Zeke started getting really excited about the job. He was amazed to learn that the fact that he spoke both German and Korean could be a real asset in this job. That odd combination of languages also made him believe that he had an excellent chance to get the job. So when he didn't get it, he came to my office, perplexed.

By then I had received all of the feedback from the interviewer. "I'll tell you exactly what happened," I said. "Basically, another student simply kicked your butt in preparing for this interview." I explained how that student came to me three or four days before the interview and assertively pumped me for information. I gave him the names of two previous co-ops, and that student called them up with all kinds of terrific questions: What did they think about the job? What were the supervisor's pet peeves and priorities? What qualities would be most important to emphasize in the interview? Heck, what would the interview be like?

That candidate walked into the interview already knowing a great deal about the position, and he proceeded to have a great conversation about the job rather than going into it knowing a few paragraphs off the job description.

To his credit, Zeke put that lesson to use within a week, beating out several candidates for an exciting new position in Florida.

He was the weakest candidate on paper, but he didn't skimp on preparation that time. He realized that you can't call a timeout in an interview if you haven't seized the opportunity to prepare in advance.

Due Diligence

Northeastern University alum Keith Laughman has had an exceptional career as a co-op and full-time professional since graduating in 2002. However, back on his first computer-related co-op job, he made a mistake that made him wonder if he had just ruined his future with his employer. Instead, it turned out to be a valuable (if painful) learning experience for him.

I remember my first solo project as a co-op in a Fortune 100's Information Technology department. We had a huge, sophisticated computer network, and we were responsible for all the servers, storage, and backup. I needed to make some upgrades, and it was no small task.

I spent all morning and the early afternoon preparing the scripts and files that I needed, making sure I had the process nailed down. At 2:00, I went to the datacenter and began the process. The first step was to shut down the servers affected by the change. One of the most overlooked tasks in any datacenter is the labeling of servers, hardware, and peripherals. So I started to search around for the right servers: I noticed that some of the labels were worn down and doubled up on each other.

You can probably guess what happened next. As I started my migration and shut down the two servers, I could hear a distinct increase in the number of calls that were flooding into the computer room phone in the background. "Man, something must have just happened because that line only rings when there are problems," I thought. "Oh well, at least it's not me."

I was about ten minutes into my changes, when two other

administrators came running through the door shouting at me. After I explained my situation, I was promptly shown that I had in fact shut down the wrong server. I thought I was just shutting down the new server involved in my changes. However, the new hardware contained other servers too! So I actually had shut down two other servers. The next thing I knew the director strolled in and asked why she was getting calls about our crucial SAP database being down in all of North America!

As if I didn't feel bad enough, I then realized I also had shut down the application servers for North America. What that means in laymen's terms is that we could not take orders from any retailers in North America. I had caused a massive data outage in the middle of the business day. Even though the datacenter was chilly with the air conditioner, I was sweating bullets. I thought I had ruined my chances of coming back to this job. After correcting the issues, we were able to get the servers back up and running–just in time for the close of business.

But there are a couple morals to this story. First and foremost, you always need to perform all tasks with due diligence. Whether you are working within IT, finance, journalism, nursing, or engineering, you need to understand the consequences of mistakes and "first do no harm." When employers give you responsibility, you need to know how to handle that. I have seen many co-ops, interns, and new hires come and go: Some of them think that the datacenter is nothing but a giant lab, a plaything. That perception can lead to major mistakes.

The greatest lesson that I learned from this company and my co-op experience was that it taught me how to handle my tasks responsibly and recognize the fact that I am working in a major company. What I learned that day I have used as a benchmark for all subsequent production changes, migrations, and upgrades that I have ever done.

One of the other things I learned was a lesson in effective management. You might recall that the director paid me a visit in the datacenter. I thought for sure I was going to get it when I saw her. Luckily for me, the reality was just the opposite. She shared a story with me from early in her career, when she brought down a mainframe for another Fortune 500 company. Then she asked me what I had learned from that day's mistakes.

When I told her, she was very compassionate. We talked about some things we could have done different to make sure everything was all set for the migration. She had told me that working with a production environment as large as ours, it is easy to get wrapped up in performing blind tasks: Part of being an efficient employee is to exercise caution where needed. You had to analyze all angles and learn to anticipate problems.

It's not like fixing a PC at home. When you make any changes to the environment in an IT department, you are affecting many users globally and not just the immediate people that support the box. What I took out of discussion was a deeper sense of who I am affecting, and this made me much more holistically aware of the how dramatic the consequences of my actions can be.

I felt terrible about the outage because I had to pull in several of my other team members to help me fix it, thus taking time out of their schedules. Although they were pleasant about it, it was up to me to prove that I had taken the risks into play for future changes. I had to earn some of the respect back so that they would give me 100% trust again when the time came to make another change.

The qualities of compassion and understanding my manager demonstrated have been character traits that I look for in managers everywhere I go. Not only that: I also try to instill those exact qualities into my peers and the people I train. It is much easier to talk to someone when they can understand your situation and relate their own experiences to it.

The High Road

My former student Michelle George eventually became a manager supervising other co-op students who worked with me. Michelle tells me that all were impressive, but she remembered one small moment that she thought was minor but exceptional.

Her student—"Lucinda Locke"—got a phone call from someone who worked at the same company. This individual was known as a highly intelligent guy but severely lacking in social skills. He needed a software application on his computer, and Lucinda started explaining why there might be a problem in making that happen. He interrupted her, saying "Look, I don't care... Just get me the *[bleeping]* piece of software."

Lucinda wasn't fazed by the harsh, inappropriate language. She just went to Michelle and matter-of-factly repeated what this internal customer had said to her. "She really wanted to solve the problem first," Michelle recalls. "I had to say, 'Okay, great... but I'm going to have to address his behavior with him or his manager. That's not acceptable.' But what really impressed me was that she didn't get rattled."

When you're a young professional, eventually you're going to see—or in this case, hear—things that are inappropriate and unprofessional. It's important to stay composed. You can't control whether people act and speak professionally, you can only control your own behavior. Sometimes young professionals get sucked into lowering their standards by emulating the bad behaviors that they see around them. You always want to be able to look back and feel that you held yourself to a high standard—even if those standards are considerably higher than those of a co-worker.

A Snap Decision

Molly Simpson, a marketing student in the College of Business Administration at Northeastern University, told this story to my first-time co-ops when I had her speak as part of an upperclassmen panel in my Professional Development for Co-op course in Spring 2006. Less than an hour after the class, one of the students in that class e-mailed me. She wanted me to thank Molly for telling this story. The student said that she had received a job offer and agonized about whether or not she should accept it. After hearing Molly speak, she knew that it would be a mistake to panic and accept a job despite significant reservations about whether it was a fit. So not only did Molly learn from her mistake—someone else did too! Here is Molly's story:

As a second-year business student starting my first co-op search, I found the process rather confusing and most of all stressful. Often I felt as though I wasn't doing things fast enough or getting responses soon enough. The deadlines were looming constantly, and my co-op advisor often was telling us, "Okay, this week you should have accomplished this task, and next week you should be hearing from that person."

I needed a job for early January, but by the middle of November I had nothing. I didn't know how worried I should be and felt as though things needed to be going faster. I had one interview which went okay: Surprisingly, I got a call back for a second interview. That went okay as well. I was a little uneasy about things, though: I had never been on co-op before so I didn't really know what to expect. Two days after that second interview, I got a voice mail in which they offered me the job. With no thought process involved, I called back and accepted. In my mind, I was thinking that being offered the job meant that it was a foregone conclusion that I would accept. I also had nothing else: no other interviews, no other job offers. So I just took it.

Later that week I went in to speak with my co-op advisor. I told her that I had accepted the job. She knew already and then asked me if it was what I had really wanted. "Sure it was," I told her. "I had nothing else so I didn't really have any options." She explained that I did in fact have options and that in the co-op process it was actually early. I felt a little more uneasy about the job, but I knew that I had accepted the job. It was my responsibility to complete the six-month work term, as I had said I would.

At first the job went rather well. I liked what I was doing, the people I was working with, and the paycheck. As time went on, though, things got a little worse and eventually turned around completely. It got so bad that just coming to work was a chore: It even wore on my self-confidence and self-esteem. It was such a bad fit that I ultimately realized that I had not worked at my highest output level mostly because I was so uncomfortable in that atmosphere.

Today, I look back on this experience as one where I learned a great deal about myself, what I like to do, and most of all the people I like to work with. I have become more cautious and thorough when deciding what jobs to pursue. During the interview, I also interview the company to see if it will be a good fit for me. I also learned to trust my intuition about the organization and the people and most of all to wait, be patient, and not make snap decisions that may solve the immediate problem of getting a job but which can cause more substantial problems in the long run.

Sympathy For the Interviewer

I remember doing a practice interview with "Kevin Cartier," just a few days before his first major interview. The job was with a big accounting firm: They hired students to work in Florida, providing them with good pay and free housing in furnished condos just a few miles from some beautiful beaches. Suffice to say that Kevin wanted this job very badly.

Kevin had a great GPA and really looked to be a great match for the position. The problem was that his interviewing skills were really poor. No matter what question I asked him, he immediately started blurting out a response and raced through it as fast as he could.

Afterwards, I gave him his critique. "Watching you interview is like watching a cat scramble up a tree," I told him. "You don't really think about where you're going, and the next thing you know you're out on a limb, wondering how you got there and how you're going to get down."

"But I thought the idea in an interview was to answer any question right away," he said. "It just feels awkward if they're sitting there waiting for you to answer."

I told him he had a great point. "Three seconds of silence feels like 30 seconds when you're being interviewed," I said. "But to the interviewer it just seems like three seconds. If you're asked a tough question, don't be afraid to take several seconds to think it over. You can even buy yourself time by saying, 'That's a good question' or by asking a clarifying question in return."

I also tried to explain how hard it is to be on the other side of the interview. "Think of all the balls that the interviewer needs to keep in the air. You need to know what questions you're going to ask. You need to evaluate each answer and decide whether a follow-up question is needed. All the while, you've got to be evaluating the candidate, taking notes, and *digesting* everything that the interviewee says. You talked so fast that I really had trouble digesting much of anything in your interview."

So we worked on *using silence in the interview.* We practiced having him slow down for harder questions, and then we worked on pausing briefly after he made each strategic point. "Think about the best lecturers that you have in the classroom," I told him. "How fast do they talk? And how often do they just stop and let you think about what they said?"

Kevin worked hard on these stylistic issues. Of course, he got the offer for the great job in Florida. Afterwards, I asked one of the interviewers to tell me about his interview. "Oh, what we really liked about Kevin was how he was very *thoughtful* in replying to our behavioral-based questions," she said. "He didn't rush into anything; he really thought before he spoke. We thought his judgment was really good."

I almost burst out laughing. I really wanted to say, "You should have seen him about three days ago!" But they didn't need to know about that. The next time I saw Kevin, I praised him for his coachability and openness to criticism. He had accepted some feedback despite the fact that it initially seemed counterintuitive to him, and it paid off in a hurry.

Hope For The Best; Prepare For The Worst

Several years ago my student "Nathan Englert" very badly wanted a particular job with a professional sports team, and there was a reasonable chance that they might hire him. After he went through our usual work on the resume and practice interview, I sent his resume out in early November for a job that would start in early January.

I didn't hear from Nathan for six weeks. During the busiest weeks of our interviewing process, my usual philosophy is to help those who seek help and not worry about those who don't stay in touch: I figure that either they are all set or that finding a job is not a high priority.

So finally Nathan turned up in my office in mid-December—just a few weeks before he was supposed to start work. When I asked him where he had been, he said he had been waiting to see if that sports team would call him: After all, that was his first choice.

I told him he had made a mistake: Our motto in job searches is always "Hope for the best; prepare for the worst." Nathan did a great deal of the former but none of the latter: That job had been filled weeks ago! Now I had to tell him that it might be too late to get a job at all. He seemed very irritated when I told him this, but I let that go; I figured he was just mad at himself. We agreed on some other possible jobs, and I sent out his resume.

I heard about another job a few days later and thought it might be plausible for him. I called him and left a voice mail for him on his cellphone. Within a half-hour, he called back. Much to my surprise, he was very angry. "When you called me before, I was right in the middle of an interview!" he exclaimed. "It was really awkward when my cellphone went off right when I was answering a question. I don't appreciate that." With that, he hung up on me.

I was too astonished at first to be angry. But the more I thought about it, I couldn't believe that he had the gall to be upset with *me* because *he* forgot to turn off his cellphone! Unbelievable. I waited a while until I cooled down and then I sent him an e-mail. By then it was a couple of days before Christmas break. I told him that I was really astonished at his unprofessional reaction to my message. I mentioned how fortunate it was that I had called instead of a potential employer. If he was going to blame others for his own mistakes, then he could look for his own job as far as I was concerned. I would still give him credit. I just wasn't about to have him work with my employers if he was going to have these temper tantrums. Lastly, I told him to not be impulsive in replying to my message: I would not check my e-mail account until January 2, so he would be well-advised to think long and hard before deciding whether he could work with me as a professional.

When I got back in the office, there was a long and apologetic e-mail. He finally understood that the issue was not really him versus me: It was the fact that his interactions with me had to be treated as an audition for the professional world. Several months later, he told me that he had been diagnosed with depression, and that was linked to some of his anger management issues. He worked hard on overcoming that illness and waited a while before going on co-op again. By then he had grown up to a remarkable degree. He finished up with a hugely successful last job and was always amazingly good at owning responsibility for his successes and shortcomings from then on.

Life Of A Salesman

Tyler Harvey, an Environment and Business major at the University of Waterloo in Canada, has managed to earn outstanding evaluations on all of his co-op jobs as an undergraduate. Pulling this off in his last co-op job was especially impressive: His primary responsibility was doing something that made him quite uncomfortable.

Tyler was a Research Assistant for a corporation that worked for a public hospital in Ontario, Canada. His job was to convince heart patients to enroll in a clinical trial. Bear in mind the following: The individuals he approached were heart patients who already needed to have a needle stuck into the femoral artery—a large blood vessel near the groin. This is an important procedure, but it also has medical risks associated with it. As you might imagine, heart patients and their family members aren't exactly excited about the idea of a big needle in the groin area.

Still, Tyler's job was to approach these individuals and ask them if they would be willing to endure a *second* needle in the same region. He needed to sell them on the idea of having a needle put in the femoral vein to go along with the artery. And what was the benefit for the patient? Nothing at all: It was for research purposes only.

"I was very nervous approaching people," Tyler admits. "I could hear it in my own voice. I didn't really know the procedure and had doubts about whether I could answer the questions that might arise. Often family members were there, and that only added to my nervousness. I felt I was intruding on their day."

Fortunately Tyler had the sense to go to the lead investigator and sub-investigator of the study to discuss his discomfort. He was able to convey that he wanted to do the best possible job as well as his concerns that he wasn't cutting it. "I've never done this; it's new to me," Tyler told them. "I don't know all the risks."

The investigators thought it would be helpful for Tyler to see the procedures, and he jumped at the opportunity. "I satisfied myself that the risks were minimal and not greater than they would be otherwise [when doing the required procedure]."

Still, the job was difficult. "People are already nervous about the procedure, and I'm asking them to double their risks: Some days you ask five people and get five rejections," Tyler says. When that happened, "I had other tasks that I could focus on."

However, those "other tasks" were mundane duties—at least at first. "I honestly would try to take on whatever responsibility they would give me. I learned protocols, did data entry, and went along with doctors and nurses when they enrolled patients in studies."

Earning the chance to take on bigger and better things didn't happen magically... or immediately. "I don't think I was doing it consciously," Tyler says. "I'd just rather be busy than bored. So I would talk to my supervisors to get more work, and whatever I was asked to do I would do well. They could see I wanted to do as much as possible. There was no exact turning point, but I noticed that they started saying 'Okay, Tyler, you take this one' when it came to some tasks."

While concentrating on doing those jobs to the best of his ability, he also changed his attitude toward the salesmanship element of the job. "I was personable about it," he says. "I was being a salesman but not approaching it that way. I was successful because I would just tell them honestly what the study was about, and I learned enough so I could answer the questions that would come up."

This co-op turned out to be a great example of how a job can teach you what you *don't* want to do with your career. "I learned I don't like being a salesman," Tyler says now. "I don't like forcing people to make decisions when they have possible negative ramifications."

Like a real pro, though, Tyler did a great job of controlling what he was able to control in the job. He did everything he could to master the job, learning through observation and dialogue with his supervisors. Most importantly, he never let his discomfort keep him from getting a terrific evaluation. "I was worried about how well I was doing," Tyler said. "But when I approached the investigators, they said I was doing better than anybody had previously."

The lessons from this job were simple. "Personally, the biggest thing is to approach every situation positively, even when the job isn't necessarily what I want to be doing," he says. "Any task can help you progress and continually get better at your job. That's the key to being successful. Another key is knowing your strengths and weaknesses: You need to keep working on your weaknesses, telling people when you're not comfortable in a situation."

When you don't settle for being adequate in a job, you can surprise yourself by getting a great review in a job that is outside of your natural comfort level. That certainly separates the true professionals from the wannabes.

The World Doesn't Revolve Around You

One challenge of working with college students is that I need to help them make the transition from student to employee. Given that they are paying a good amount of money to go to a private university, some of my students really act like customers when interacting with anyone on campus. While that is somewhat understandable, I try to get them out of that mentality when they start working with me. After all, when they go out for their first job, the *employer* will be the customer.

"But I'm supposed to be *learning* as well as getting paid, aren't I?" some students ask occasionally. Absolutely, that' s true. But first things first: As a paid employee, you need to do what that employer needs you to do. My wife's cousin Chris Parker—who was a co-op at NU Law School many years ago—told me about interviewing several potential new hires at his law firm. All were asked, "What would you most like to work on here if we hire you?" The guy who got the job was the one who said, "I'd like to help you handle your biggest need, whatever that may be."

Unfortunately, some students have trouble letting go of that customer mentality as they start making the transition to the workplace. Years ago, I began working with a very serious, rather uptight Asian-American student who I'll call "Natalie Xiu" for our purposes here.

When I conduct a practice interview with a student, I'll typically start it several minutes after the required time. It's interesting to see how that affects interviewees: The good ones just quietly focus on their interview strategy, mentally rehearsing ideas that they want to convey or reviewing notes. The less-prepared ones sometimes find any delay almost unbearable: Their anxiety level really skyrockets.

So I brought Natalie into my office around 11:07 for an 11 a.m. interview. "Sorry to keep you waiting," I said as I ushered her into my office.

Natalie glared at me. "I'm really mad that you made you wait," she said angrily. "My time is important to me, and I don't appreciate it."

I was momentarily stunned and then became quite angry as well. But I also recognized an opportunity to turn this exchange into a learning opportunity for Natalie. "You have no idea why you were made to wait, do you?" I said. "It could be because our computer network crashed, and maybe dealing with that is more urgent than interviewing a co-op. It could have been because I just got an urgent phone call and learned that a family member is critically ill.

"But I'll tell you why you were forced to wait all of seven minutes today: It was a test to see how you could handle a little inconvenience. And you *flunked* that test."

I was tempted to just cancel the interview at that point but decided to just see what would happen. The tensions gradually faded. When asked about her weaknesses, Natalie talked about her temper—which I took as an apology of sorts.

Afterwards, we had a pretty unemotional conversation about what had happened. I asked her why she reacted that way, and she said that it often was an effective way to get things to happen on campus.

This surprised me. "How do people usually react when you blow up like that?" I asked her.

"Usually they try to calm me down," she said.

So it definitely was a case of making sure that she knew that acting like a disgruntled customer was not going to be acceptable as a job seeker. "I can't afford to have you throw a temper tantrum at Gillette just because the interviewer happens to start the interview late. It just won't fly."

She got the message and went on to have a successful career. In fact, I only heard one mild complaint from one of her supervisors: Natalie didn't like to take breaks. Even when they were celebrating a co-worker's birthday, her boss had to twist her arm to get her to take a few minutes to have some cake.

So her serious and uptight personality never did change, but that wasn't the issue. She just needed to realize that the world of work would not revolve around her.

San Diego Blues

Several years ago I worked with our entrepreneurship students at Northeastern. Seniors had the option of doing a three-month co-op for Winter quarter or taking a brief vacation before finishing up during the Spring. So one of my entrepreneurship students came to my office and announced that he was going to waive his co-op. He had an ambitious plan: He was going to use the three months to go to San Diego, find a temporary job, AND find a full-time job for after graduation. I told him that he could do this as an "experiential co-op" if he kept a journal and wrote a lengthy paper.

Three months later, I had those in hand, but they certainly weren't what I expected. The whole experience had been painful. He never found a temporary job OR a full-time job. He spent most of his days fruitlessly looking for work and most of his nights feeling sad and lonely and far from home.

Eventually some painful truths smacked him in the face. He realized that he had been full of bravado with not much substance to back it up: For the last few years he had indulged in a lot of big talk about starting a business doing—well, something—and making lots of money. Alone in San Diego, he faced the unpleasant truth: He didn't have any capital to start a business and probably would not be in a position to do so for at least ten years. He hadn't put any energy into developing meaningful relationships, and as a result he didn't have any. He had decided it was time to change his priorities.

We met after I read the journal. "Well, as you can see, the whole thing was just a disaster," he said. "Are you kidding?" I said. "I think you learned more on this co-op than on all of your other ones put together!"

A Missed Deadline

Inevitably, things will go wrong in your job—and some may be beyond your control. Mistakes are made, obstacles arise, and all kinds of things can come up that may make it impossible to complete something to the best of your ability by an agreed upon time. Once it happens, you can't change things like these: So how are you going to handle them? As this story by "Sherrie," an alum from the College of Arts and Sciences at Northeastern illustrates, you actually can gain considerable respect from peers and supervisors if you are honest, timely, and professional when communicating about an unanticipated problem.

As a law clerk in a Washington, DC firm, I was working late through the night with a young associate on a time-sensitive project. I realized we were not going to be able to finish, despite our exhaustive efforts. I called the lead partner the day *before* it was due and left a message stating the impossibility of meeting our deadline. I then listed the various things that we collectively had agreed to finish in the next two days, and our estimated completion date.

I was careful to ensure that my tone was apologetic, but firm. I knew I had to come across as confident, decisive, and in control—not meek, defensive, and especially not nervous lest the partner fear that we were not in control of the situation.

He called back a half hour later. He said that what I had done in communicating our status, our action plan, and our estimated completion was *exactly* what I should have done. He thanked me for my initiative and told me to keep up the good work.

Subsequently, I overheard this partner tell others that I will be an excellent attorney when I "grow up" (meaning when I finish law school). I truly believe that legal skill and analysis is merely one part of what he meant. The ability to communicate effectively, persuasively, and succinctly goes beyond the courtroom: It matters *every day*, on every task, whether menial or sophisticated. This experience has taught me that a successful person does not trivialize the small things. Trite, I know. But these small things add up to a bigger thing called integrity—the true mark of a successful person and professional.

CHAPTER SEVEN

Build Relationships

When I was working toward my MBA, I took a class with Boston University Professor Tim Hall. It was a career development course in the discipline of Organizational Behavior (OB).

Some of my peers in the program had ridiculed me for my interest in OB. "It's not very *lucrative,*" one fellow student said to me in a condescending tone. Regardless, the subject matter was interesting to me... and this class proved to be a fascinating and challenging course.

Basically, we had to write a short autobiography. We needed to keep a detailed diary of a work day and a non-work day. We completed numerous tests and surveys, including the Myers-Briggs Type Indicator (a personality test) and the Strong-Campbell Interest Inventory, which compared our preferences in life and work to those of numerous professionals in a host of fields.

After that, we had to analyze all that we produced and create a list of themes—elements that surely needed to be components of our careers. By the time the course ended, I had produced a 65-page project. And I had concluded that the two most critical themes were that writing and teaching needed to be significant parts of my career.

It was one of those courses that I knew would influence my career for a long time—but that happened much more directly than I ever could have anticipated. Several months later, Professor Hall happened to be the speaker at my MBA convocation. He gave a terrific speech revolving around an analogy. He talked about cormorants as birds that are talented fishers but also very greedy. As a result, fishermen had long exploited these two traits by attaching each cormorant to a line and putting a metal band around its neck so it would catch fish but be unable to eat them. The fishermen would enjoy the spoils, and the cormorants would keep working hard to catch more fish.

Professor Hall then likened the cormorants to us MBA graduates! We were talented, yes, but perhaps more greedy than the average member of the population... and thus readily exploitable.

It was a terrific and even brave speech under the circumstances, so I went up to Tim afterwards to commend him on it. Just making small talk, he asked me what I was up to. As it happened, I had been hired by a local psychologist to edit his book. "Oh, right, I remember that you have strong writing ability and a great interest in it, too," Tim said.

I thanked him and moved on to the celebration. But he called me a few weeks later. "I remember that you were doing some sort of writing project, and I wondered if you'd be interested in taking on another one," Tim told me. Apparently he and a co-author had been asked to revise their Human Resource Management textbook to make it current. Would I be interested in the job? I was thrilled and worked on it for the next month or so.

Around the same time, I was looking for my first real job after getting my graduate degree. Having taught in the public schools with some success, I thought I'd like to try my hand at teaching OB to college students. I wrote to almost all of the programs in the Boston area and got nowhere. But I hadn't tried my alma mater yet, so I gave a call to Jan Wohlberg, who supervised the OB teaching assistants under Professor George Labovitz.

My goal was to secure an interview. I told Jan I was interested in teaching, and she asked what my background was. I mentioned that I was in the process of rewriting Tim Hall's HRM textbook. "Well, if you're good enough for Tim, you're good enough for us," Jan said. "Can you teach this September?" I was shocked! All I wanted was an interview, and now I had a job without even needing to interview. And it was all because of my relationship with Tim Hall.

After working at BU for a few years, I wanted to branch out to other schools. I dropped by to meet Andy Priem, the head of the HRM group at Northeastern. The result was the same: I just mentioned my work with Tim and then my more recent work at BU, and I had my first job at Northeastern—again, without any real interview. I don't know if I ever would've ended up in academia without that connection from a luminary in the field.

Of course, it's almost impossible to make a decent living as a part-time lecturer at universities, so I talked to Tim about other career opportunities. He suggested a few consulting companies in the area. Again, that personal connection made all the difference. I was hired as a management consultant for a company that specialized in interviewing great and not-so-great employees at various companies. I analyzed interviews and wrote up the best stories to show trainees what a great performer looks like in action.

As I described in the introduction of this textbook, that process of analyzing stories for themes has come full circle with the completion of this book.

It all began with my relationship with Tim Hall. I made a strong impression in his class, continued making efforts to find opportunities to write and teach, made the most of those chances when they came my way, and then stayed in touch with my mentors after moving on to other pursuits.

You never know the final destination of your career, but the relationships you build along the way are critical to both your enjoyment of the journey as well as the distance you are able to travel in maximizing your success.

The Seventh Key – Build Relationships

The seventh key to professional success is to build relationships. Lawyer, civil rights activist, and Washington power broker Vernon Jordan said:

"You are where you are today because you stand on somebody's shoulders. And wherever you are heading, you cannot get there by yourself. If you stand on the shoulders of others, you have a reciprocal responsibility to live your life so that others may stand on your shoulders. It's the quid pro quo of life."

Chris London is the founder and editor-in-chief of Manhattan Society.com, a philanthropic organization devoted to building "a greater sense of community and charity in New York City." London says:

"Networking with integrity creates a greater willingness of all parties to be part of a human conduit to serve as energy and resource to one another. Sometimes you will give more than you receive and sometimes you will get back more than you give. It's not about keeping score."

Management guru Peter Drucker said:

"More business decisions occur over lunch and dinner than at any other time, yet no MBA courses are given on the subject."

I have found that some young professionals tend to overrate the importance of technical talent and task expertise while underestimating the value of interpersonal skills. If you ask most people what their job is, they are likely to tell you that they design buildings, make financial decisions, and so forth.

Your knowledge and experience certainly are important in opening doors, but your ability to build relationships often determines whether you get much farther than the front hallway. Successful professionals vary greatly in terms of personality profile, but one common trait is that most of them have figured out how to forge alliances within and beyond their organizations.

You might be the very best individual contributor in your organizational role, but if you alienate people because you're a "high maintenance" individual and/or someone who is unwilling to go beyond your own responsibilities, you may have a difficult time advancing much beyond your initial job. Conversely, getting people to believe in you—based on your attitude as a team player as well as your individual performance—can make all the difference in whether your career progress accelerates or stalls.

Elements of Building Relationships

In scrutinizing stories featuring themes related to building relationships, I derived several sub-themes that comprise this key to professional success:

1. Treat others as you would want to be treated.
This harkens back to The Golden Rule. If you approach your interactions with others in a way that reflects a low level of interest,

they likely will respond the same way. The reverse is true as well. Sometimes when I conduct practice interviews, I intentionally come across as a bit negative. But when the interviewee is not flustered by that and responds with positive energy, I find it almost impossible to maintain that tough, negative persona—even though I'm just pretending!

If you take interest in your colleagues and their success—even when it's not really your responsibility—they are far more likely to do the same for you. The best relationships are mutually beneficial ones in which everyone wins.

2. *Work at understanding others' needs and personality differences.*

Eventually you will encounter colleagues who present you with two forms of difficulty. One issue is that there are many different types of personalities, and some of them may be the opposite of yours. For example, you may be a worker who prefers an unstructured work environment in which you go with the flow. But if you have a boss or co-worker who loves structure—making lists, wanting to have regular planning meetings, and so forth—you would be wise to bend a little to accommodate their needs. If you can respect those individual differences instead of being frustrated by them, you're well on your way to building a good relationship.

A second issue is that most workplaces of any size have at least some individuals who are just difficult, period. In those cases, it may take extra effort to figure out how to work with someone who is demanding, negative, complaining, or unreasonable. It's best to not take the treatment personally, as you may have no idea what's causing the person to be that way. Try to avoid escalating negative energy. Focus on tasks and results. You may not turn around every tough individual, but you may avoid getting derailed or distracted by this kind of person.

3. Strive to earn credibility—even in small steps.
When you're first hired, your new supervisor and co-worker usually will have positive or neutral expectations about how you will turn out as an employee. It's nice to have instant respect and credibility, but you shouldn't assume that you do. Credibility is something that you earn a little at a time. Getting to work early, going the extra mile on a low-level task, showing some interest in the work of others—all these are good starts toward accumulating that credibility.

4. Be careful to avoid anything that affects the degree to which you are trusted in the workplace.
If credibility usually accrues a little at a time, it certainly can slip away at a much faster pace. As we saw in the "Do The Right Thing" chapter, any number of behaviors can erode trust. It might be failing to own up to a mistake or being caught in a small lie. It could be an inexplicable lack of communication when you needed to be late or absent, or when a problem arose in handling a situation.

In some instances, some young professionals end up being a little *too* successful in building relationships. Going out to lunch or maybe even a drink with colleagues might be harmless, but it also could be the first step toward a relationship that is a little too intense when you're relatively new to a work environment. It's great to build relationships, but sometimes it's best to move slowly.

True Stories about Building Relationships

Marathon Man

When I first started working with Wai Man "Tony" Lam as he looked for his first co-op job, I envisioned him being one of the last students to find a job. Tony had about a 2.3 GPA and absolutely no corporate experience. His best job had been working as a cashier at the John Hancock Observatory gift shop before it closed down.

He was quiet and didn't have a very dynamic personality, and he did poorly on his practice interview.

Much to my surprise, he managed to get an interview with one of my better employers—a fluke, in my opinion, as there wasn't much on his resume to justify it. Even more strangely, they actually hired him. I was very surprised but obviously happy for him.

When I visited him on the job a few months later, it all became clear. Tony had one of those "moments of truth" arise during his job interview—just one quick exchange that made all the difference. His manager told me that Tony's interview had been nothing special. It was obvious that he didn't have much in the way of skills. As almost an afterthought—just going through the motions of finishing up the interview—the manager asked him, "What pay rate would you be seeking from us?"

Tony looked down and thought long and hard. Then he looked up and said, very seriously, "For the opportunity to work in this organization, I'd be willing to work for the minimum wage."

"My heart kind of went out to the kid," the manager told me. "I said, 'Well, we would never pay someone just minimum wage, but I'll tell you what. We've listed the job as $10-15 an hour. I'll offer you the job for $10 an hour.'"

"That was a really nice thing that you did," I said.

The manager gave me an odd look. "Nice had nothing to do with it," he said. "This guy was so obviously hungry to learn. Now he's our Webmaster."

Tony didn't miss one day of work and earned an outstanding evaluation. For the next interview cycle, I went ahead and told employers that Tony was not a flashy personality or great at interviewing but that he now had proved to be a superstar in the workplace. Gillette hired him to provide PC support at all levels of the organization. Ironically, the qualities that were such a negative for Tony in interviewing turned out to be a real asset in the position. The end users at Gillette liked him because he wasn't arrogant or condescending—even though he knew more about computers than they did. He quietly helped them out in a modest, unassuming way.

Tony was one of only about 20 students university-wide who won a Co-op Award as a senior. This is given to students who have earned terrific evaluations on all of their co-op jobs and truly exceeded expectations in the process.

Tony was the last person I would have expected to win, based on my first few meetings with him. It just shows that the classroom is a sprint, while a job is a marathon. Some people are strong in both, but some are weak in one but great in the other. Tony was a champion marathoner.

One Honest Interviewee

My former colleague Mike Ablove told me a great little story about the value of honesty in interviewing. Now, you can imagine that employers get a little weary of "smokescreen" answers in interviewing—especially when they ask someone about their weaknesses. Some students think it's great to say that they're a workaholic in answer to this question. There are two problems with that. One is that many struggle with the follow-up question that asks "Why is that a weakness?" Another is that a savvy interviewer may worry that you're saying this because you don't want to tell them one of your *real* weaknesses. So it's really not great to use a pseudo-weakness to answer this question.

Mike worked with a very overweight young woman who was asked this question by one on-campus interviewer. When she was asked about her weakness, she offered a one-word answer: "Chocolate." The employer burst out laughing and said, "That's the first honest answer I've heard all day!" He ended up offering her a job.

If that seems too simplistic to be true, think about it. She gained some credibility by being honest, but she also showed a sense of humor as well as self-awareness and a comfort level with who she was. All of these traits are more important than most job seekers realize.

Building Visibility

For many years I've enjoyed working with Barbara Murphy, who works in Human Resources for the Corporate Information Technology division at The Gillette Company. Barbara has terrific tips for aspiring young professionals. One opportunity she recommends volunteerism—especially if the co-op or intern is a technology-savvy member of the millennial generation. "If the company offers an in-house education program and volunteer instructors are needed, co-ops do a great job here as they have expertise, especially technical expertise, and they get to hone their presentation skills while building visibility," Barbara says.

Some other tips: "Ask for more responsibility, take notes, manage your manager, be sure to get face time with your manager, find a mentor." By managing your manager, Barbara means that you have to be proactive in seeking additional responsibilities and useful feedback on top of figuring out your supervisor's idiosyncrasies.

One former co-op she remembers was particularly good at building visibility: Barbara tells me that she's passed along the Bill Mayo story "a million times."

Barbara used to hold midway point check-in meetings with the many co-ops who worked at Gillette in Corporate Information Technology (CIT). At one of those meetings, Barbara reminded Bill Mayo's group that those seeking full-time employment with the company should bear in mind that managers always planned their budgets for the next year in the fall. This meant that September could be an opportune time to initiate conversations about future employment.

Bill had been working on making himself visible with the company's decision-makers. He did a great job on a presentation to upper management around that time. The upshot was that Bill capitalized on the window of opportunity. By December—well before many of his peers even had begun interviewing—Bill already had his position approved in the budget; he was lined up for a job when he graduated in June.

But Bill didn't stop networking at that point. He thought it would be great to take advantage of the fact that Gillette is a multinational company. Bill wanted to work overseas. He made sure that people knew about this interest, and—sure enough—he ended up with an overseas assignment for over a year.

Once Bill returned to the company's corporate headquarters in Boston, his next role was in Internal Audit as Director of Worldwide Systems Audit. That job was a direct result of making sure that the company's Chief Information Officer (CIO) knew he was interested in such a role. While in *that* role, Bill managed to become a part of the IT leadership team, which gave him an opportunity to cultivate relationships with more senior managers—which led to yet another new role with the company!

It's hard to underestimate the importance of building visibility—whether it's as a co-op, intern, or new hire as a young professional. In fact, Barbara always tells me that it's the visibility of Northeastern students that gives them the job-market advantage over graduating seniors from many prestigious universities in the greater Boston area. "I'm sure we could hire great people out of Harvard, MIT, Boston University, and so forth," Barbara always tells me. "But it's so hard to tell how good someone really is from a 20-minute interview. When we hire a co-op who's worked for us for six months, we have a very good idea of their strengths and needs for further professional development.

"I figure that if we hire ten co-ops, probably nine of them will do a great job and help us get work done that needs to get done now. If three or four out of those nine end up as such superstars that we hire them when they graduate, that's a pretty good batting average," Barbara says.

Another factor for Gillette and many other large corporations is the cost of making the *wrong* hiring decisions. Many of these employers have to go through a long and cumbersome process to terminate an employee—even when it's pretty obvious that things aren't working out. Companies have to document what has gone wrong and often hold "coaching meetings" to give the poor performer every opportunity to turn his or her performance around. The end result is still usually a termination, but this process minimizes the chance of a lawsuit from a disgruntled employee who has been fired. Of course, it's still very costly in terms of time, energy, and morale.

With all of this in mind, it's good to think of a co-op or internship—or even the first six months of a full-time job—as a "six-month job interview." You always need to keep proving that you can justify having the company make an additional investment in you as a valuable human resource.

From Rookie To Veteran

Back in October 2003, I made an announcement to my Professional Development for Co-op class. I had an employer who needed part-time help in a Finance/MIS role right away, and there was a good chance it could become a full-time co-op down the road. To my surprise, only one student showed any interest. Amanda Roche stepped up and got the job.

With no real professional experience, it was daunting for her to begin her first job with a big financial services company in a Boston office tower. "I had never had an office job before, and I didn't know what the culture would be like," Amanda recalls. "What could I do to prepare myself? How should I act? I was anxious but excited."

Nonetheless, it didn't take long for her to start making connections in her new job. "They just throw you into the middle of it," she says. "But I learned to establish relationships with the people I worked with. I always helped people who needed help, and that gave me exposure. I got positive feedback for that."

Next up was figuring out when to ask questions. "Initially I thought I shouldn't because it would make me seem clueless," she says now. Basically through trial and error, she learned that some of her co-workers were terrific resources, while others lacked the ability and/or willingness to be of much assistance. That helped her determine who to go back to in the future.

Her next challenge was working with a boss who had too much on his plate. "My boss has an attention span of about five seconds. So I learned right away to condense my questions and make them as clear and concise as possible. My approach is 'Here's a problem; here's what I think we should do; what do you think?' He's there to guide me, but he wants me to think for myself and have a plan when I go to him."

A typical situation came up when Amanda was asked to get signatures on contracts that can be up to 25 pages in length. "The department heads would always have questions, so I figured out that we should make cover sheets for the contracts that highlight what the contract is, the background, purpose, terms, cost, and people who are being charged. Then I made places for the signatures on the cover page." This procedure saved everyone time and helped Amanda build credibility with her many internal customers as well as her boss.

When I first visited Amanda's boss, he told me that the company's Chief Financial Officer had told him that Amanda was the best direct report in her group—even though she was the only co-op!

"If you ask me to do something, no matter what it is, I'm going to put in 110%," Amanda says. "I'm looking for exposure and experience. There's always so much more to learn about market data. The more projects I participate in, the more I'll know, and the better off I'll be."

Extra effort combined with a knack for building mutually beneficial relationships has been the key to Amanda's success. "It's not just about what I need," she says. "It's a two-way street. If something needs to get done by the first of the month, we need to cooperate and work together to make it happen. I don't just need their help; they need my help."

As I write this in June 2006, Amanda has worked for the same employer either full-time or part-time almost non-stop since October 2003, and she's going back for her third co-op with her very appreciative employer this summer. It's going to be interesting to see future employers try to figure out how someone managed to get over three years of professional job experience in a five-year program. A total natural when it comes to managing her work relationships, Amanda has shown that even the least experienced employee can surpass the performance of many people who have years of experience. She was a co-op rookie less than three years ago but now is a seasoned veteran in the corporate workplace—and she won't even graduate for another ten months!

Critical Care

For many years I served on our Co-op Awards Committee and heard many remarkable stories of above and beyond performance by students across our university's many colleges. Typically, my own students from the College of Business Administration were blown away when they heard about their counterparts who worked in the health sciences.

One of my all-time favorite stories is about a male nurse—a guy who had played football in high school—named Michael, as I recall. He worked with critically and even terminally ill pediatric patients at a local hospital, and the head of the hospital received two amazing letters from parents about this co-op.

One letter was from parents who talked about the nursing co-op's work with their young son, who was scheduled to undergo multiple surgeries. He was terrified. The aspiring nurse came up with a brilliant solution. Knowing that this boy was absolutely obsessed with his Sony PlayStation, Michael explained how the operating room was set up just like the PlayStation and how as a patient he got to be right in the middle of it! By the time the surgery rolled around, the young patient was genuinely excited to face it. His parents were incredibly grateful.

An even more poignant story came out of something else that happened on his co-op. Michael was involved with the care of a terminally ill adolescent boy. One morning, Michael noticed that the boy seemed very depressed. This seemed understandable for someone who had weeks, maybe months to live. But Michael assumed nothing and learned through a casual conversation that this patient was unhappy for a reason that any healthy adolescent could understand. He thought his hair looked stupid.

Some might have shrugged this off as inconsequential under the circumstances. Instead, Michael made a few calls and arranged for a Newbury Street hairdresser to come in and donate a free and extremely stylish haircut.

The boy did die as expected. Afterwards, his parents wrote to the hospital to commend this young nurse and how his extra efforts put a smile on their son's face when he desperately needed a lift.

The 100-Degree Factory Floor
As the following story written by Mary Rose Tichar at Case Western Reserve University illustrates, the best young professionals realize how critical it is to develop relationships with individuals across all levels of the organizational hierarchy, even when it entails getting your hands dirty... and sweaty!

Mechanical engineering student "Ellis Hawthorne" did not obtain a co-op the first time he applied. The second time wasn't looking so great either. A very fine young man, Ellis couldn't figure out where he fit in with mechanical engineering.

A local manufacturing company needed a mechanical student, and I asked them to at least interview Ellis. Honestly, I had my doubts about the company being a good fit for Ellis. But Ellis was hired and spent the first month in the manufacturing facility—fine for a new co-op, except that it was very hot that summer. He worked in a dirty, loud environment with temperatures over 100 degrees.

Ellis looked at this situation as an opportunity to develop what he called "important relationships" with the laborers. The employees at this company are often foreign and relatively uneducated, but Ellis said, "They know a whole lot more than I do about the process and product." With that attitude, he quickly won the respect of the laborers. Ellis refers to his time on that factory floor as important and an essential complement to his later work on the computer in the air conditioned office.

The president of the company called me one day and raved about Ellis and his ability to work with everyone at the company. He asked me to please send more students just like Ellis—willing to work hard, develop relationships, and make significant contributions at all levels of the organization.

Relationship Wreck
Although it's critical to build positive relationships with co-

workers, some young professionals can end up making that too much of a priority. My co-op colleagues Jacki Diani and Mary Carney talked to me about a particularly distressing example of this.

There are many pitfalls that can arise on the social side of work. The tricky part is that many situations can seem pretty innocent at first glance. What could be wrong with small talk at work about what you did on the weekend? Is it such a bad thing to go out for a few drinks with colleagues after work (assuming that you're of legal drinking age)? Could there be any harm caused by chatting at work about your love life, your partying habits, and so forth?

Not necessarily—but sometimes problems occur. Jacki and Mary warn their students that they may be just making a bed or putting away supplies in a health care environment, but it's always possible that a patient or family member may overhear the conversation. How are they going to feel about the quality of care if they learn that some staff members were out getting drunk or dancing the night away well into the night before?

Even in a corporate environment, small talk might be just friendly banter... but depending on the content, it could raise concerns about professionalism or the degree to which the job is a priority.

A nursing co-op that I'll call "Lucy Evans" didn't *think* that she was headed for trouble with colleagues on her co-op—quite the opposite, in fact. She worked in a large, urban teaching hospital with very sick patients and staff members who were stressed, but many of the full-time staff were about her age and very friendly to boot.

Lucy made friends quickly, and a small group started going out after work a lot. In particular, Lucy made a close friend of one full-time nurse. Just weeks into the co-op, Lucy basically had integrated her new friend into her most intimate social circle. Her full-time counterpart met Lucy's boyfriend and a whole bunch of Northeastern students. They even went on vacation together.

But then something happened that ruined the friendship. Jacki never did find out what it was, and perhaps it doesn't matter. Just like that, Lucy's work environment changed dramatically. Her former close confidante stopped mentoring her and treated her coldly. The great relationship that initially was a valuable coping mechanism in a stressful work environment now actually added more strain to her days.

It got worse. Her ex-friend went to a supervisor and accused Lucy of "falsifying the documentation of vital signs." A Nurse Manager broke the news to Lucy and made it clear that she believed her ex-friend's version of the events, even though Lucy strongly proclaimed her innocence. The Nurse Manager suggested that she could grieve the matter or resign.

The atmosphere had become "malignant." Lucy chose to resign.

"I don't think we'll ever know what really happened," Jacki said. "It's just a real sad way for things to end."

Talking to first-time students about the situation, Jacki and Mary try to emphasize that it's great to build relationships at work but that it's best to proceed with caution. "Students may ask, 'How will I know if I'm doing the right thing?' when it comes to making friends at work. It can take two years to really get to know someone," Jacki and Mary tell students. "In this case, the cost was high. She can't work at that hospital again in the short term at least, and it's a great place to work."

Unsurprisingly, Lucy's reflection paper dealt primarily with all that she reluctantly learned about the working world because of what had happened with her "professional buddies." In her paper, she wrote: "I should have gone to the manager and co-op advisors. That is where I went wrong; I had the resources and did not use them."

The Difficult Co-Worker

Ali Ciccariello was in my Professional Development for Co-op class in Fall 2004, and she continues to amaze me with her terrific attitude. In her own words, here is a story that she shared with me from her job with a large financial services company in Boston. Her story is a great example of how much work it can take to forge relationships in the workplace—especially when everyone else is telling you how impossible a given person is!

I've found that dealing with difficult people at work is far more challenging than dealing with difficult people at school. At work, you can't complain to your boss about people the way you would to a teacher, and you can't remove yourself from the team you're working on. Confronting a difficult person at work is also tricky. If you say the wrong thing and offend them, you'll be forced to work in an awkward situation until either you or the other person leaves.

A few months into my co-op, I began having issues with a woman who was a full-time employee at the company. She worked with me indirectly; her role on my team was administrative. Basically, she was in charge of executing all the changes I needed to make in the database we manage.

All of my co-workers had problems working with this woman. She liked doing things her way. In fact, her way was the *only* way things would get done. When we had meetings with her, she would interrupt people, have an attitude, or simply avoid making the changes we had asked her to make. My co-workers treated her the way they felt she was treating them—with little respect.

One day, this lady became so difficult to work with that I was on the verge of tears. I had asked her to complete a change for me, and all I got in response was an attitude. I honestly felt like this woman hated me. I tried talking to my co-workers, but nobody had any advice for me. When it came to dealing with this individual, they were all in the same boat.

The other dilemma that resulted from this small "tiff" was a real worry to me. Without this woman, I couldn't complete the project my boss had assigned to me. How could I go back to him and tell him I was unable to finish my project because I couldn't work with others?

I went home that night and thought about how I usually dealt with this woman. I tried to put myself in her shoes for a minute. How would I like it if someone half my age was telling me what I needed to do and when I needed to do it? Also, I reflected on how I had delivered work to her. I think I had an attitude of "Just do this" versus "Could you please help me?" Maybe I hadn't shown appreciation for the fact that this woman had worked at my company longer than I had and knew more than I did about many aspects about this field.

When I went back to work, I changed my attitude toward her. I try to take a little more time to show appreciation and get her input instead of attempting to delegate tasks to her. By doing so, my boss has told me that I now have developed one of the *best* relationships with her in the office.

When dealing with people, it's easy to get caught up in your own needs and tasks. Figuring out to how manage my relationship with this difficult co-worker showed me how critical it is to try to put yourself in someone else's shoes and ask, "How would *I* want to be treated?" if the roles were reversed.

Friends In High Places

When she started her first corporate job, my former student Michelle George tells me that she felt "awestruck, like I was meeting a rock and roll star." With most of her previous experience coming from a job in an ice cream shop, it was intimidating to work with seemingly omnipotent businesspeople.

Some of the "joking" comments she first heard at her job didn't exactly make her feel more relaxed in her young corporate career. "I remember one Director saying, 'This soda might be bad. Let's get a co-op to try it!'" she recalls. "You get the mindset that you're stuck in the worst possible place. Maybe you're in a closet or a really bad cube."

But Michelle found a way to turn her mindset around. "You have to start thinking of yourself as a real employee," she says. "You think that you can't associate with these people because you're just a co-op. But you can. I started assisting people in other groups on the floor—accompanying them on service calls."

By helping out another co-op of mine in this other group, Michelle developed a relationship with that co-op's manager. In time, that directly led to her next job. This just kept happening for Michelle. Every job she had exposed her to more and more managers at the company. She didn't always work directly with these managers, but her group interfaced with the various managers' groups. As a result, word of her upbeat attitude and strong performance got around.

A year or two after graduation, Michelle faced a family situation in which it suddenly was important for her to increase her earnings dramatically. She came to talk about it with me. She had her eye on a position within her company, but it was *four* salary grades above her current role. How could she make herself a legitimate contender for that job? We worked on interviewing strategy for a while—and quite a bit on just building up her belief that she really *was* good enough to compete for the job—and she had a strong interview.

But would that be enough in light of the big jump that this would be for her? Michelle is convinced that one of those managers whom she barely knew—but who definitely knew about her through the connections she had made by being friendly and supportive to people across groups—must have put in a good word for her to tip the scales in her favor.

Getting that phone call from Michelle with the stunning news that she had secured the job and obtained a $20,000 raise was a real career highlight for me. It also is a great reminder that any young professional can build a network of contacts though sheer effort both on the job and in making an effort to befriend and assist as many people as possible in their work environment.

EPILOGUE

Mastering The Seven Keys To Success

When I teach the required Professional Development for Co-op course to Northeastern University business majors, I sometimes begin the class by asking students to complete a survey featuring 18 statements. For each, the student must decide whether they strongly agree, agree, neither agree nor disagree, disagree, or strongly disagree with the statement.

Some of the survey items are intended to assess how confident and comfortable the students are feeling before they begin the course and their first job search through Northeastern. These statements ask students to reflect on what they already know about writing resumes, interviewing, and the job search process. A typical statement would be "I am nervous about going on co-op."

Other survey items are meant to help me ascertain the values and expectations of the students. I ask them to comment on their willingness to do low-level work to get ahead, whether or not they view their parents as primary role models, and so forth.

When we first administered the survey to almost 200 students back in Fall 2004, a few results really stood out to me. Roughly 56 percent of the respondents "agreed" or "strongly agreed" with the statement "I am nervous about going on co-op." Simultaneously, almost 90 percent of those surveyed "strongly agreed" with the statement "It's important to me to achieve great things in my career and my life." That was a rather eye-popping figure to me.

But while the magnitude of some numbers proved surprising, the survey still gave me statistical validation of something I had suspected for a while. Given that we are a university that is renowned for its cooperative education program, we tend to attract young adults who are willing to work and remarkably achievement-oriented. Yet these terrific traits sometimes are combined with considerable anxiety. Commonly, aspiring professionals wonder whether they really have what it takes to be successful working full-time hours over several months in their field.

When I set out to write this book, I hoped to accomplish two goals. First, I have to acknowledge that I have seen many young professionals struggle with the transition to the workplace. Therefore, I hope that this book will make workplace newcomers more aware of what it *really* takes to be successful. Secondly, though, I want to convey the idea that exceeding expectations does not require superhuman capabilities. In fact, I'm willing to bet that you have demonstrated at least some of these qualities even if you have *never* worked in a professional environment.

In that same Professional Development for Co-op class, I do an exercise in which students are required to write up true stories about themselves. The stories might be from menial jobs, school, personal situations—anything, really. I have them write up roughly five of these stories that they ultimately can use in a job interview. The instructions are to write stories about their greatest successes and their most difficult challenges—not too different from the stories that we included in this book, except that they rarely are from professional settings. So here's one more story for you, a personal favorite. As you read it, try to see how many of the seven keys to professional success you can identify in the story.

The Losing Streak

Amanda O'Brien is a finance concentrator at Northeastern University, class of 2008. She wrote the following story about eight months before beginning her first co-op job.

My senior year in high school I played Varsity Basketball. My team had a reputation of not being very good, and few fellow students made an appearance at our games. The team members were beginning to bicker and blame each other for our losing streak. Our coach struggled to keep the team together, and many players turned on him, too. Each team member had a different reason for being jealous of a teammate. Whether it was younger members took their position or because they thought others did not work hard enough in practice, it hurt the team's performance on the court. I knew that a transformation had to come from within and that it was my job as a senior to take the first step.

I remember one particular team meeting the day before a game. We were two weeks away from the playoffs and needed to win three out of the next four games to secure a playoff spot. As my teammates continued to bicker, I stood up and began to draw a diagram on the white board. I drew a stick figure representing each teammate and slowly everyone stopped talking, wondering what I was doing. Their attitudes immediately changed as they laughed at my lack of artistic ability. I then explained that although our team was made up of individuals, the basketball team is a single unit. Each game we had played, whether we won or lost, was something we all took part in. Many players felt we were losing because they were not getting enough playing time. It had become the team consensus that our coach was incompetent.

I stressed to them that no matter how good or bad of a job our coach had done, the way we play as a team was not his fault. The fact that everyone was playing for themselves was not a result of his bad coaching. I explained to them how much time and effort he put in and how playing Varsity Basketball was more than just a game. It was a privilege. We owed it to everyone who put their time and money into our team to play as a team—whether that meant all the sophomore players starting or each player working a little harder in practice. The players began to put their heads down, ashamed of their previous actions and comments. I said that we need to make a pact as a team to disregard what anyone had said to another team member that may have been hurtful and to agree we were all sorry. We talked about putting what had happened in the past aside and looking forward to the upcoming game. The team put their hands together and cheered.

From then on, we took our season game by game and practice by practice. Everyone worked to change their attitude and outlook on the team. We did win the game the following day and ultimately made it into the playoffs. Although we did not win the championship, we had a great time playing together and I felt that everyone grew personally as a result.

Later that season both my coach and the Junior Varsity coach thanked me for the courage I showed standing up to the team and the leadership I showed as a player and person. My coach nominated me for a sportsmanship scholarship and upon graduation I found out I had received it. In front of my class of 500 I was awarded the Salem High School Sportsmanship Scholarship, an honor I still appreciate today.

Reflections on "The Losing Streak"

If I had to choose a chapter in this book for this story, it probably would be "Chapter One – Own Responsibility." The pivotal element of this story for me is the fact that Amanda stood up and took an unpopular stand, demanding that her teammates join her in taking charge of being successful—or failing—as a team.

However, this story also shows someone *staying positive* amidst considerable negativity. It demonstrates a person who was determined to *do the right thing* even when that behavior contradicted the mindset of the group. Amanda had to get her teammates to *see the big picture* and change their perceptions of what it meant to be to have the "privilege" of playing varsity basketball. She also exemplified the *control what you can* key by implicitly acknowledging that they couldn't change their coach or their own past behaviors. Amanda absolutely needed to *build relationships* with her teammates—or rebuild them, perhaps—to get everyone on the same page. All of her efforts certainly could be characterized as culminating in having the team *exceed expectations*, and Amanda earned a cherished award as a result. Essentially, then, this story shows all seven of the keys to professional success.

If you reflect on or reread all or part of this book, you'll find that most of the stories show individuals demonstrating at least two or three different keys in any of the situations. That's very significant for a few reasons: First, it brings home the point that any great success that you have as a professional usually proves that you have *several* great qualities, not just one. When Amanda Roche showed how to *own responsibility* upon making a major mistake in her story back in Chapter One, she also made a major step in her efforts to *build relationships* with her supervisor and co-worker. Plus, she showed how to *control what you can*: It may have been too late to undo the mistake, but she learned not only from her mistake but by reflecting on how others had not managed to *do the right thing* in similar circumstances.

There's another reason why I included Amanda O'Brien's story in this epilogue. Right now you may lack professional experience, but I'm certain that you already have demonstrated at least some of the seven skills in school, in a menial job, or while engaged in a sport or other extracurricular activity. So start thinking about your own "moment of truth" stories. Write them out, making sure to focus on something *specific*: your toughest class, your greatest personal challenge, your hardest day or week in a specific job, the most difficult customer that you handled successfully, and so on. With practice, you'll have great stories that can be used in job interviews to show employers what qualities you have to offer.

And if you have some good stories now, it's also important to think about the kind of stories that you will *want* to be able to tell *after* those critical early jobs in your professional career. Seize the opportunities that you have to exceed expectations in the workplace, just as you read about in this book. By now I hope you'll appreciate that many of these opportunities are disguised in the apparent form of "bad jobs," difficult co-workers, and extremely challenging circumstances. The top professionals find a way to accept and overcome these obstacles. If you do it right, you'll develop an autobiographical anthology of success stories.

Mastering the Seven Keys

It's no accident that this book's subtitle is *Mastering the Seven Keys to Professional Success*. Many stories in *Exceeding Expectations* are from my experiences on the cooperative education faculty at Northeastern University. Before I ever put them on paper, I had collected many of them over the years and often used them to bring to life key points when working one-on-one with students or teaching the Professional Development for Co-op class.

While this has been effective in showing small groups of students some of the keys to success, I am excited about sharing these stories with a wider audience of young professionals. In that sense, I hope that this book serves as a "master key" to help you unlock the mysteries of organizational life on the road to personal and professional success. Good Luck as you strive to exceed expectations!

DISCUSSION QUESTIONS

1. This book lists seven keys to professional success. Which of the seven do you think will be easiest for you to demonstrate in the workplace? Which will be the hardest? Explain your answer by providing examples of when you have shown one of these qualities and when you have struggled to demonstrate another of the qualities.

2. In chapter one, there is a story called "The Victim Mentality." Re-read that story and react to it. In your experience, have you known individuals who have this mentality? If it's not a productive outlook on life, why do so many people seem unable to own responsibility and change this aspect of themselves?

3. In chapter two, there are several stories about people who somehow managed to stay positive despite repeated failures and seemingly hopeless situations. Whether in school, work, or some other aspect of your life, describe a specific time when you managed to stay positive in the face of significant adversity. Be sure to include plenty of details about what happened step by step to convey exactly how you did this.

4. The third chapter of the book revolves around exceeding expectations. When you have managed to go the extra mile in a situation, what was it that motivated you to go above and beyond? Describe how you exceeded expectations—whether they were your own or others'.

5. Chapter three has many stories about exceeding expectations. Citing at least three specific stories from that chapter, describe at least three specific ways in which you now intend to go the extra mile in your next job.

6. Chapter four focuses on doing the right thing when facing conflicts, ethical dilemmas, or unfair treatment. If you became aware of a co-worker doing something wrong at work—sexually harassing someone, falsifying a time sheet, or making a potentially costly mistake—what would determine whether or not you would talk to a supervisor about it? Would it depend on how friendly you were with the person who was doing wrong? How costly the issue would be to the company? Are you the kind of person who can't keep quiet if something is wrong, or do you usually figure it's none of your business?

7. In chapter five, the author claims that "seeing the big picture" might be the most difficult to master of all seven principles. Do you agree or disagree? Discuss at least three stories in chapter five in justifying your answer.

8. Describe a specific time in which you made a significant short-term sacrifice in order to gain something greater in the longer term or bigger picture.

9. Chapter five has two memorable stories about individuals who went to great lengths to begin careers in the music industry and sports management. What would *you* be willing to sacrifice in order to secure a place in the organization or career of your dreams? Would you work full-time hours unpaid? Would you work 70-80 hours per week or more for low pay? Why or why not? What qualities are most important to you in a job?

10. Chapter six talks about the need to "control what you can" in the workplace, including learning from your mistakes. Discuss a specific situation--from school, a job, or a personal experience--in in which you made a mistake that turned out to be a valuable learning experience for you.

11. The final chapter in the book emphasizes the need to build relationships. Based on what you read in this chapter, describe at least four ways in which you could build relationships in the workplace in order to benefit your career.

12. There are over 80 stories in this book. Discuss *four* stories that had the biggest impact on you in terms of developing your understanding of what it *really* takes to become a successful professional in the workplace.

About The Author

Scott Weighart is a Senior Coordinator of Cooperative Education on the faculty at Northeastern University. He has been working with co-op students and employers since 1995. Author of *Find Your First Professional Job: A Guide For Co-ops, Interns, And Full-Time Job Seekers*, Weighart has appeared on network television as an interviewing expert and delivered workshops on co-op topics and the millennial generation at local and national conferences.